I was Hurt But now I am Healed

By S.E. Gardner

Avid Readers Publishing Group

Lakewood, California

I Was Hurt But Now I Am Healed

Avid Readers Publishing Group

http://www.avidreaderspg.com

ISBN-13: 978-1-61286-230-9

Printed in the United States

What makes me victorious?

My courage to climb

This book is dedicated to all the girls and boys who held in their tears as their screams were muffled. Those who were too scared to talk and thought that it would be easier to be an adult than to cry like a baby; and who never let anyone see the tears behind their smiles. This is for the ones who never wanted to look like a coward and fought their battles in silence. Feeling as if they never had protection but, found out they were stronger than their attacker in the end. This is for the ones who had no family to run to. This is for the family members who thought it was easier to turn a blind eye than face the truth.

I was with my future husband one day in the bed. We had been dating for a few weeks and were still in the process of getting to know one another. That night we were in the middle of making out and was about to become intimate. While we were in the process I had a flash back in my mind and my whole demeanor changed. “What’s wrong with you” he asked me. “Nothing” I replied. “Did someone do something to you? Have you been raped or something”? And after a long pause I said “Yes. I spent my whole life holding it all inside and when I have a flash back I don’t know how to control myself.” He leaned and wrapped me up in arms and asked if he could hear my story because I didn’t have to hold it in anymore. He was here now to listen to me and protect me from all harm. So instead of being physical and intimate, we became emotionally intimate, I told him my story. Not only did I have a person in my life that was willing to listen to me but I had a person in my life that paid attention to the change in my behavior. Even when I tried to hide it and say nothing was wrong he corrected me quickly and told me it was. He asked that I tell him what the issue was “I see it all in your eyes. When I touched you something was not right. Your eyes can’t lie to me” he told me. My own parents didn’t see the signs but this person whom I had known for just a little while knew something was deeply wrong with the woman that was laying in his arms. And that I was hiding something inside that needed to be set free. He knew that if I didn’t set it free that he would end up paying for past pain that I have not faced. He held my hand to let me know I was not alone while gently running his fingers through my hair. “Talk I’m ready” he said. With tears in my eyes I let out my story. Here it goes….

Part 1: In the eyes of a child

There's a monster in my bed

There's a monster in my bed as I go running to my mother arms showing her
Fear that only a mother eye can see but she was blinded and she can not see
There's a monster in my bed

There's a monster in my bed as I grab my father's arm to me he is the
Strongest man in the world but he is tired from work and his eyes are blurry
And he can not see there's a monster in my bed

There's a monster in my bed as I hug my grandmother but she is to busy complaining
About how she doesn't like my mother and I am a child her eyes can not see and she
Doesn't care if there is a monster in my bed

There's a monster in my bed and I'll face it alone and close my eyes and drift off to a
Far away world untouched and a secret place that only my eyes can see while there's
A monster in my bed

Today must be a bad day it's raining hard and all I can hear is thunder. I really don't remember why I didn't have school today but I am stuck at home. I am looking out of the big front window in the front room. Playing on the good furniture you know the furniture that is covered with that nosey ass plastic covering. And is only sat on when company comes over.

Its morning time but the storm today is making the sky look so dark almost like night time. I hate the dark and today is the day I can remember why.

They say you can't remember anything under the age of six. Well that's bullshit! I can't remember what age I am exactly but I know for a fact I am younger than six. I remember this day all the time and I play it back in my head all the time second by second minute by minute. Sometimes I cry and sometimes I get mad at myself. But should I be?

I am not exactly sure what day it is. I don't know if it is a Monday or Friday I just know there is no school today and I am alone with him. I think it is Fall or early Spring time I am not for sure what season it is or what month. I see the big tree in front of our house with no leaves on it all the leaves are on the ground. It's not winter time because there is no snow outside but it's cold. I live on a street called Northland a big green house. When I look at this house now as a grown woman I want to burn it down to the ground but that won't bring me happiness and it won't heal me. There are no happy memories of this house once I think about my childhood and how this pain started.

I use to like lightening before today. I use to love the way it lit up the sky. My daddy would tease me and tell me that God was coming to get me because I was bad and that is why the sky was rumbling. Now when I see lightening in the sky and hear the rumbling it does nothing but make me replay shit in my head that I can't erase. There are nights when we have lightening storms and I don't sleep not because of the lightening but because of the memories they bring back. But if I fall asleep before the lightening storm then it's a good night for me and whoever is in my life at the time.

The lightening streaks across the sky look so pretty to my innocent eyes. Here he comes to sit next to me and we began to look out the window together watching the rain fall and the lightening flash across the sky. The furniture is covered with plastic. To make sure it is always clean when company comes over to have drinks. The big old tree seems to reach to the sky. I remember on this day is when I seen a lighting strike something for the first time. There was a big rumble then a lightning bolt hit the big tree at the top and part of it fell to the ground. It pulled down the power line in front of our house and the street was blocked off.

We both watched it in amazement and I screamed when the tree was hit by the lightening. Was this the beginning of a bad omen? Now there is no power and the house is dark and quiet. The only sound is the thunder the only light I see are the streaks in the sky.

My best friend is Cleo she was my first dog. My daddy brought her for me when I was first born. My daddy loves me he will buy me anything I ask for except for ice cream off of the ice cream truck. He always tells me we have ice cream in the house you can eat but there is just something special about getting it off of the ice cream truck. He always makes sure I have everything I need before I ask him. Except for one thing and that was the ice cream off the ice cream truck. I would get so mad at my dad when the other kids would run to the truck to get ice cream and I couldn't. That is the only thing I wanted because I couldn't have it. And when I got older and could buy it myself I wondered what is the big deal about this ice cream? It cost a lot more than the ice cream at the corner store. But I just had to have it.

He is still here I don't know how old he is but he is with me a lot when my mommy and daddy are gone to work. He has always been with me since I can remember. I think he is my brother but I don't know what a brother is. People ask me is that my brother I say yes but what is a brother? Since I don't know I just say yes what else could he be? Is a brother a bad thing to have? My mommy never told me what a brother is. I know his name and I call him by that.

I go to a little school in a big church on a busy street there are a lot of cars and buses on this busy street. I don't know the name of it right now but I know my daddy works way down the street from my school. There are lots of kids my size there I don't remember their names but we all play together. One day I will go to the big school by our house. We pass it all the time but right now I am not big enough to go there. But I think my brother goes there I am not for sure.

He puts Cleo outside on the top porch I don't know why. The weather is bad outside we don't let her out in bad weather but he does today. He is big so I guess what he is doing is right. I don't understand why Cleo has to be in the rain and in the lightening but one day when I get older I will.

He calls me to his room by my nick name. I have a lot of names that I go by. My friends at school call me by my real name but my mommy, daddy and my brother call me by my nick name. Mr. Roberts and his family next door call me by another nick name. My Uncles on my dad side calls me by a nick name that have for me and my Big Momma and some of my family that is far away down south call me by a name they have for me there. I don't know why I have so many names but I do. And I answer to all of them. But when I go around my daddy's family and when I go to school they call me by my real name. My daddy's family don't have a special name for me like everyone else does.

I go to him I have no reason not to. I have no reason not to trust him. My parent must trust him they leave me with him all alone while they work. I see him lying on the bottom bunk bed in his room. He has no clothes on and tells me to get under the covers. They are red white and blue hockey blankets. But I have always seen him with no clothes on this isn't the first time. My mommy sees me with no clothes on all the time when she gives me a bath. Me and him don't have the same body. I don't know why I never asked him and I never asked my mommy why we have different bodies. Maybe that is how I will look when I get big like him. He tells me to take off my clothes. I take them off as he say. He calls me over to him and tells me to lay on top of him. I do it I have done it plenty of times before. Sometimes he rubs my body up and down on him and makes noise. I don't make a noise I just lay there. I don't know what this means but it doesn't hurt. We just don't have clothes on.

But now he takes my head and tells me to open my mouth. He puts something in my mouth from between his legs. I don't know what it is. But he does it all the time to me. If I choke he always stops for a few minutes then start again with the same thing. He would never hurt me that is why I do it. He holds my head down there. I don't know for how long I am down there. Sometimes I am under those red white & blue hockey blankets that he has for a long time and sometimes for a short time. I don't hate those blankets right now but one day when I am older seeing those blankets will unleash a ton of hate inside of me. Not only for him but for my parents as well.

He holds my head down there between his legs. He has hair down there I don't have hair yet not down there maybe when I get big like him it will come there. I wonder do my mommy and daddy have hair down there. I never asked them. But I have long ponytails past my shoulders and one of my front teeth is missing just like my Uncle. He is done I have a funny taste in my mouth. Right now I don't know what this is but later on I will find out. He tells me to go spit in the toilet or the garbage can but not on the floor or on his blankets. I do what he says because he is bigger than me and he knows what is right for me.

I lay with him numerous times when we are at home alone. We never lay together when my mommy and daddy are home. When they are home he acts like he can't stand to be around me. We don't talk when we are in his bed we just lay there sometimes I fall asleep on top of him. But he always makes sure my clothes are on when my mommy comes home from work.

When my mommy comes home she is always mad and fussing about stuff I don't know about. She comes in look at the mail or turn on the television. But she always has dinner fix before my dad comes home. If his dinner isn't made by the time he gets home from work he gets really mad at her and screams. Sometimes he drinks his stuff from his glass and go to sleep. It smells funny and I don't get to drink that. Only big people can. I don't know what it is called but there are bottles of it on my daddy's bar in the front room. I tried a sip of it once and it was nasty and burned my throat when I tried to swallow it.

This is the era where people placed plastic over their "good furniture". And it wasn't uncommon for a husband and wife to have the same hair do. The wife could have an afro and the husband could as well. Color coordination wasn't important. You could wear stripes and poka dots and be in style. And hand-me-down clothing was nothing to be embarrassed about.

I go to a big school now. I graduated from my little school. I wore a white hat and white dress with my white Easter shoes. My daddy took pictures of me holding up my special paper. My daddy took me to his mother house but she didn't seem to care about my special paper or my special hat.

I am so happy that I go to the big school by our house just like my brother. It is the biggest building I have ever seen in my life. I feel just like a big kid I have a book bag with my one little book in it. I am in the second grade at school 23.

It is almost time for Christmas but my birthday is 2 weeks before Christmas and my mom said I can have a birthday party. I have never had a birthday party before. I am going to be 6 on my birthday and my mommy said that was a special birthday and that I could have a party. I am going to tell all my friends to come to my birthday party on Saturday. This is the first birthday party I have ever had. But I didn't know that it was last party I will ever have.

It's Saturday and all the kids in the neighborhood have come over to our house for my birthday party. I never saw so many kids at my house before. My mommy and daddy never let me have friends over to play with me. When I play with my friends I always have to go outside. The party is over and my mommy is so mad at me because I told all my friends at the big school to come to my big birthday party. I did what she said why is she so mad at me? I only told 100 friends that is not a lot of friends for a 6 year old to have is it? I think she must have fussed at me for the rest of the year. She never let me have another party again.

It's Christmas time. I remember my mommy and daddy friends came over to the house. They are different than me there skin look white I don't remember their name but they have a big son named Paul he looks funny and wears glasses. Those glasses are super thick and even thou Paul is big he acts like a kid like me and we always sit in the floor and play together. They gave me a small wooden musical jewelry box. It had 3 little wooden girl figures on it with long hair like mine and a sign that read "Main Street". My daddy works on Main Street. My mommy told me not to break it because the lady made it especially for me for my special 6th birthday.

This was the best Christmas ever in all my life. I have had many Christmas before this one and after this one but I will always remember this one maybe because I had a birthday party this year. For Christmas I got a big wheel, my first doll house, a black ballerina doll, Barbie dolls I think 4 of them with clothes and furniture. And I also got skates, a desk, a big toy box, car for my Barbie dolls and dishes. I got everything a child could want at 6 during this time.

My Uncle is over. He always smells funny like pee-pee. I think he got 4 teeth but that is okay. I love my Uncle he always gives me money and candy every time he sees me. My uncle and daddy always drink stuff that taste nasty and laugh really loud when they watch Television. They always watch the three Stooges and westerns. They will watch the same old movies over and over again and laugh like it's their first time seeing it. They watch television and eat a lot of food and then sleep on the couch and snore really loud with their mouths hanging open. But sometimes daddy gets mad at mommy I don't know why he yells and screams at her. She tells me to grab my coat and we run downstairs away from daddy. Sometimes when daddy car isn't in the drive way we drive to my mommy Aunt house or walk to her house. Or sometimes she drives around crying. I don't know why she cries I just lay in the back seat and go to sleep or look out the window while we are driving. There are times when we go in the basement and just sit for a little while until she thinks daddy has fallen asleep. When we go back upstairs to go in the house mommy tells me to be quiet and go to bed. I do what she says because mommy is always right. She never tells me why he screams at her and I never ask.

My mommy stomach has been getting bigger and my daddy tells me she has a brother in there for me. I am so excited I have never been around a baby before other than my baby dolls. I know how to take care of a baby because I take care of my dolls all the time. Today my mommy is going to the doctor to get my brother out of her big stomach. I am so happy. I told all my friends that my mommy is going to the hospital to get my brother out of her stomach. It's almost time for my mommy to come get me from school I can't wait to see my brother. All my classmates will see my brother for the first time just like me. I see my mother at the door with other parents I run to the door when I see her. Rebecca comes to the door and say "where's is your brother I don't see a baby". My mommy gave me a look that I have never seen before she looked at me and I swear she killed me with her eyes. My mom grabbed me by the hand and told me "You talk too much no one told you to open your mouth". She dragged me out of the school all the way to the car. I was so hurt I never asked about my brother again maybe he is still at the hospital. I was too scared to ask where he was I didn't want my mommy to get mad at me again. I hated Rebecca ever since that day. She opened her big mouth and made my mommy so mad at me. My daddy never said anything about my brother no one did. All the happiness we had for him died at that moment and no one ever told me why and I was so scared to ask about him. When I would play with my toys I would pretend he was there playing with me and when I played with my dolls I would pretend one of them was him. Even thou I never seen him I loved him. Maybe because during the times my mommy stomach was getting bigger it kept mommy and daddy from fighting.

We live on Northland and my mommy made sure I would remember where I lived at in case I get lost. She also made me remember our phone number in case something happened I would know how to call home. So also made me remember my Ha-momma number which what I call my daddy's mother. It's my special name for her. And my mommy's mother I call her Big Momma.

It's a big green house that we live in. And we live upstairs and another family lives downstairs. There is a mommy and a girl bigger than me and she has a brother like me. He has a funny eye and wears thick glasses. And his hair is nappy it's not curly and soft like my daddy hair or my Uncle hair. I don't know how old they are but they are bigger than me. There mommy is short, chubby and light skinned her kids don't look like her. Maybe they look like their daddy I don't know because I never seen their daddy.

The brother became my friend. He would always give me the mail for me to take upstairs to my mommy. When I would sit in the hallway to play with my dolls he would like to lay on top of me like my brother does. But we don't take off our clothes and we don't go in the bed. We are always in the hallway on the floor and it's not a long time. I don't know how many times he laid on top of me in the hallway but he never hurt me so I don't think it is wrong because my brother does it and he wouldn't hurt me. And my mommy always told me big people know what they are doing and he is bigger than me so I have to listen to him like I listen to my brother. His sister has seen him lay on me in the hallway and she hasn't said anything so it must be okay for him to do it.

My brother has other friends also on our street. One is a boy with muscles he is so cute he has a sister. She is light skinned not very cute and my mommy and daddy says she acts like a boy whatever that means. But she looks like a girl to me just not a very cute girl. And then there is a boy who lives on our street he is very dark skinned he isn't cute at all and he has two twin sisters. All 3 of them look alike and they look like their mommy. My brother is always hanging out with all of them all the time. They play basketball together all the time. And they all go to the big school together.

Next door is where Mr. Roberts lives with his wife. There are so many people living in that house I can't even count. All the kids live there with their husbands and their kids. They have 4 daughters the 4 daughters have husbands and they all have kids. When you go in their house there are people everywhere. They are always on the porch laughing, drinking and playing music or in the back yard cooking. It's the house that never sleeps. How I got the nick name they gave me I will never know.

But everyone that lives in his house call me by that name and my god parents call me that also. Even when I get grown and become an adult they still call me by that name when they see me in the streets. They probably don't even know my real name.

I have my Barbie dolls I have a girl doll and a boy doll called Ken that I got for Christmas. I don't like them with clothes on. I take their clothes off. I lay the girl doll on top of the boy doll. I like doing that this makes me think about me and my brother. He is always happy when I lay on top of him. I never want him to get mad at me.

My mother Aunt is old. If my Big Momma is hundred years old then my Great Aunt must be a million years old. She is always smoking and drinking when I go to her house and asking me a hundred questions about my Big momma and how I am doing and what I am doing in school. And what my daddy and mommy are doing at the house. I go to her house sometimes to stay when there is no school and my brother can't watch me. She doesn't really have a lot of hair. She is almost bald headed and have a dresser full of wigs. She has all kinds of wigs short and long or straight or curly. She doesn't have enough hair to but a burette in. But she can cook the best egg pies in the world. She always has an egg pie for me to eat when I come over there. And if she doesn't she will take her time to cook me one while I am there. There is a man that lives there he rents a room from her. And an older man I forget his name I think it was her boyfriend. He is old too he always wear a suit but each piece is a different color. But I think he is a million years old to and when he drives he drives so slow people blow their horns and yell at us when they go around us. Maybe he is trying to save on gas I don't know. He always goes in the room with my Great Aunt when I am there I can hear the television on in the room. And her son lives there to. He is bald headed and have grey eyes. I have never seen anyone black with grey eyes. I like looking at his eyes because they are different. My mommy says he has eyes like a sneaky old opossum whatever that means. I like going into her tenant room. He has a lot of magazines in his room. He lets me look through them. We talk about space and all the pretty pictures in the magazine. It's called National Geographic and one day I am going to visit those places in the magazines. But her son is always trying to teach me how to play cards. We play cards and he always let me win I think. I go to talk to him when my Great Aunt tenant is not there and when my Aunt is busy in her room or gone with her boyfriend. But one day we were in his room playing cards. This time he closes the bedroom door and asks me to come sit on his lap to play cards with him. I feel him moving while I sit on his lap. I don't know why he is moving but it doesn't hurt and it doesn't bother me. So I keep playing with the cards with him. My Great Aunt comes and opens the door and scream for me to get out of the room and go up front. I run up front to the sit on the couch and watch television. My Great Aunt has never screamed at me before. I didn't move once I sat on the couch. I have never seen my

Great Aunt mad. I can hear her yelling at him and cussing. But I don't know why we were just playing cards. She comes up front and tells me to never go in the back rooms with them with the door closed. I tell her okay and she gives me another piece of pie. I never tell my mother about it.

I didn't understand why my Great Aunt was so mad at her son at the time. But as I got older I figured it out. After I got older and sat and thought about it I understood what happened and what could have happened in my heart I always loved my Great Aunt and was thankful for her. Because in a way she saved me and my soul from further torture. My family never had anything nice to say about her it was always negative even about her kids. But in my heart I knew that out of all that negative stuff I heard about her she did one great positive thing and that was the day she saved me from her son.

Karma is a bitch! I think Karma is a woman and she doesn't tell you when she is coming she just catch with your pants down. Well my Great Aunt son got his Karma about ten years later after the incident with me he died of AIDS. He could have had it back then who knows AIDS wasn't that popular then. If AIDS was out I didn't know anything about it. I remember when we went to see him before he died. I looked at him lifeless in the hospital bed surrounded by machines and plastic curtains. He was in a coma or sleep he didn't even know we were in the room. It had been about 5 years since I last seen him. Me and my mother and my Great Aunt went to go see him one last time. He couldn't breathe on his own and he couldn't talk maybe he was dead then and Karma was keeping him alive and replaying all the dirty shit he did in his head to remind him of why he was going to hell or maybe God was giving him time to repent so that he may make it to heaven. I tried to feel some kind of sorrow for him because he was family. But my soul was happy he was dying in the worst way possible. For his funeral I didn't even wear black. I wore the loudest outfit in my closet. It was an orange 2 piece skirt set a bright orange at that. I was 16 at the time and was able to drive myself to and from the funeral. I can't remember why my mother didn't go to the funeral with me. But wearing that orange outfit to me was a way for me to quietly celebrate his soul burning in hell. Maybe I was celebrating his death with some other females that he may have hurt in the past that never said anything. From family rumors I know he was a dirty person so I know he may have hurt someone. I know he had about eight kids but I only meant 2 of them. My Great Aunt only had contact with the two that I knew that is way I was able know them.

I could never figure out why my mother hated my Great Aunt so much. I never knew what happened between them she never really talked about it except for a few times when she would say that my Great Aunt would cook one chicken and make five grown people split it to eat or sometimes not feed them at all if they didn't bring back any money. I don't know how many relative lived with my Great Aunt. But my Great Aunt was the first to leave that old country in Mississippi and come way up north to start a life. She told me that my Great Aunt was mean to her but never went into details. And that my Great Aunt should not have been that way because she had no family here up north and she knew that. And that my Great Aunt only cared about the money she could get from people. If she was so mean to you then why would you send me to her house?

But a family member once told me that my Great Aunt use to try to make my mother prostitute for money and that is how she met my father. Now my father was a handsome man high yellow and pretty jet black curly hair and had always been a flirt when it came to women. I don't know how true this story is but the family member had no reason to make it up. And I am sure my source heard it from a parent maybe they were talking about it to someone else. You know how children always repeat what they hear. It was also rumored that my Great Aunt was a prostitute and that is how she made her money up north before welfare came into existence. My Uncle and my father but told me was a prostitute. I know she never worked well she was already a million years old when I was born. Yes she always had a house full of men when I would go visit her but she never did anything provocative around me. My parents would always say that years ago my Great Aunt always had men in her bed and that was normal for her. When I was around my Great Aunt she did nothing but the normal things. The same things I saw at my house. Drink whatever was in her cup, smoke 100 cigarettes and cuss all the time. My parents would tell me of how my Great Aunt would have 3 or 4 men at one time in the bed with her. Now at that time I didn't pay that statement much attention but as I got older and compared that statement to my source statement how in the hell would they know how many men she had in her bed at one time unless they were there paying some pussy to!

My mother never shared any good child hood memories with me they were always stories of how they had to pick cotton, fight white folks to go to school, eat scraps out of the slaughter house garbage can, go hunting for food in the woods and how every time she looked around her mother was always pregnant. Nothing in her child hood was ever happy it was always sad and miserable stories she would share. She never told me stories of her boyfriends in high school or college. She never told me how she met my dad. They both shared the same story of how on their wedding day when it was time for my mommy to kiss my daddy my mommy took off running around the church because she didn't want to kiss him. Every time my daddy would tell this story he would just laugh. And to come think about it never seen them kiss. I would see my daddy try to kiss her and she would just turn away from him or push him away. I didn't understand it then and don't understand it now. She never shared any girlie secrets with me what type of woman don't have girlie secrets even my Great Aunt who is still alive and has to be about a billion years old now in the present time still had girlie secrets. And her one secret she shared with me when I was an older teenager "If you have pussy you will never go broke". That is not an understatement it took me some time but I figured out how to use her statement to my advantage when I had to.

We are moving off of Northland and moving to a street called East Delevan I don't know why we are moving but we are. We are moving up stairs again and there is no carpet on the floors. The floors are hardwood and shinny and there is a fireplace. The people that live downstairs are the landlords and they are white. One is a mother and the other is the daughter. We can't use the driveway or the backyard. They have ducks, chickens, dogs and cats back there in the yard. Sometimes the old white lady downstairs let me feed the ducks with her. My mother doesn't like it here because she says the white people down stairs are always complaining. I remember her car got hit twice on the street while it was parked. And she mad because they could not park their car in the drive way like the land lord does.

Next door is a girl she is bigger than me and light skinned I think we are around the same age she is just taller and bigger than me. My mommy says she is half white whatever that means. She is very tall taller than her mommy who is skinny and brown with short hair she has a jerry curl in her hair. But her daughter hair is black and long it's very long like mine and curly. She has a lot of Barbie dolls and sometimes we sit on her porch and play with them. And next door to her is another girl she is bigger and older than me and her. She lives with her grandmother. She is always asking me about my brother she is so nosey and ugly. Her hair is short and she a Jerry Curl in her hair as well. All these black folks in world got that Jerry Curl juice dripping everywhere. All over their clothes so you rather have juice dripping all over your clothes than wear your own hair type with no juice dripping? As my parents puts it "These black folks what white hair so bad they wanna run around here with that shit dripping everywhere".

Its summer time I think. There is no school today and I am at my new house on East Delevan Street with my brother. He is bigger now and taller than my daddy. He drives my dad big truck sometimes. I think he plays basketball somewhere around the corner for our house at the neighborhood recreation center. He also has a job around the corner from where my daddy works. He is in high school now but I don't know what grade he is in.

One day when he was watching me he tells me to come to his room. The walls of his room are blue and he has pictures on the walls from magazines and some he has drawn himself. He is a very good artist. Everyone always talk about how good he can draw. I like to draw to but I cannot draw well like him. He can draw animals and people just like they look I wish I could do that. He tells me to come lay down on the bed with him. I do it. We have done this plenty of times before but today will be something different. He pulls out a magazine and I see girls big like my mommy on the pages. But they have no clothes on. I see women showing their booty and they have tits tits like me but much bigger. Some have hair between their legs and some do not like me. My brother lets me look through the pages while he takes off his clothes. We lay in his bed and he takes his fingers and put them between my legs. I remember I started to cry because it hurt me. He yelled at me to lay there and be quiet. Cleo my dog was outside on the front porch barking. He always made sure Cleo was outside when we went to his bedroom.

I was scared he had never hurt me before or yelled at me. Somehow I managed to be quiet like he asked and lay there while his fingers were between my legs. After he took his fingers out, he grabs my head and pushed it down there between his legs like he always did. But today he must be mad at me because I am choking and he won't stop. When he is finished he screams at me to go to bed and sleep. He lets Cleo in and she jumps in my bed and lay next to me and I fall asleep.

By now a few days goes by and maybe a few weeks I am not sure. I do know that it was a long time before he calls me back to his room again. When I go I don't make a sound I just lay there and do as I am told. I don't want him to be mad at me again or yell at me. It is only pain and I can take it for a little while.

I am too young to understand what medicines can really do to you when you take them. But at this age I am old enough to know that when you take them you go to sleep. My mommy gives me medicine when I am sick and I always feel better after I wake up. And when I am sleep he doesn't call me to his room. And for some reason if I am sleep and Cleo is in my room he won't come in there. I can't remember if she ever bit him or not but he knew not to touch me when she was around. I think maybe I am around the age of seven or eight. I know I am in the third grade and I catch the big yellow bus to school with my friend. He is short, light skinned, fat and has braces. He gets off at my bus stop and makes sure I get in the house and then he walks home four blocks away. He gave me a school picture of him during picture time. He was wearing a grey suit smiling and showing off his braces. He had a little bush on his head looking like a little man. I never knew why he went out of the way to always make sure I made it on and off the bus every day. I never asked but no matter the weather he was always there waiting on me. When we would get on the bus he would always have me sit next to him even thou he was in a higher grade than me. That always made me feel so special. But as we got older I never ran into him again. I knew what high school he went to I even knew where he lived but we never saw each other.

We won't be having school for the next couple of days. I can't remember why maybe it's spring break because the weather is nice outside. But I know I will be alone with my brother and I don't want him to hurt me like he did the last time. So before I go to bed I go into the bathroom. And

I get the aspirin that mommy give me to feel better and daddy's cough syrup medicine. I take a few pills I can't remember how many and then I pour the cough syrup in the spoon and take a few spoonfuls. To make sure my daddy doesn't know I took his cough syrup I put water in it to fill it up to where it was before. I go to bed hoping to sleep a long time and not wake up until my mommy comes home.

I remember my dad fussing when we lived in this house "They want you to pay all this dam money for this cough syrup and the shit taste like water". No one ever put it together. It's funny how things can happen right up under your nose and be right in your eye site but you can't see it. How can one day your cough syrup taste like medicine then a week or two weeks later taste like water? So he went from taking cough syrup to taking cold pills instead. I couldn't mess with the pills because he would know that someone was taking them so I decided to leave those alone. But I did take my children aspirin and I did take Tylenol pills and whatever else I could take without anyone knowing. I even began sipping liquor and adding small amounts of water in its place. It burned my throat when I drank it so I only used that if I had nothing else to use. Too me that was my only form of safety going into a deep sleep. Not telling my parents not telling a teacher not telling another relative not even telling a friend. My safety was sleep and I did whatever I could to go to sleep.

Growing up my parents would always say to me "all you do is sleep when you don't have school you are so lazy". I had formed a drug habit around the age of seven or so. I was a pill popper and a cough syrup junkie and later on I would start drinking alcohol on a regular around the age of 13. My mother never questioned why the baby aspirin and Tylenol was always running out. And why was daddy cough syrup always low when no one in the house was sick. Or why did the cough syrup taste like water. She never took me to the doctor to see if I had a disorder. I was just labeled "lazy" by them. My first memory of a doctor visit was when I was 15 years of age. Before then I never went if I did which I doubt I don't remember the visits. I went to the eye doctor on a regular because I wore glasses and I went to the dentist a few times as a child the visits I can count on one hand. I think about it now and both of my parents worked all the time. I know we had health coverage. Just because I looked healthy and normal doesn't mean I was healthy and normal on the inside. If it walks like a duck and quack like a duck then it must be a duck right? Wrong! Is it normal for a child to sleep like a zombie all the time? I am not for certain that my brother did not touch me while I slept. And I honestly don't put anything past him. Maybe I was so drugged up I didn't know he was there. I knew I didn't want him to hurt me again. And getting away from the hurt met to sleep as long as I could.

We are moving again. We have lived on East Delevan for almost a year. This time to a big house and no one will be living there but us. It's our house we own it and my daddy brought it. The back yard is so big the whole house is big to me. My daddy brought me the prettiest bed set ever. Everyone got a new bedroom set and we got all new furniture to. I love my daddy. My new home is now on Cornwall Avenue. Cleo is happy she has a big yard she can run in. Not like before when she only had a small space on a balcony. Me and her can play outside in the grass and run up and down the driveway. We never got a chance to do that before now unless my daddy took us to the park.

Its summer time not sure of the exact date but its summer. But I think I'm around the age of 9. I am at my Ha-momma house well that is what I call her. She is my daddy's mommy and every now and then I go to her house sometimes too stay until my mommy gets off of work. They are family and you are suppose to love your family. Why because they are family well who ever came up with that idea was an asshole!

Ha-momma was very light skinned. So light she could pass for a white woman maybe she was white I don't know. She was fat very fat and would always get stuck in the chair when she sat down. Sometimes she would ask me to help her up. I noticed I was always treated differently when I went over there. Even as a young child I knew I wasn't really welcomed in their home I was tolerated. She lived with her daughter and her boyfriend. Who was married to another woman at the time but was living with them. In the living room there was fancy furniture and photos of family members. But no photos of me, my dad, my mom or my dad 2 brothers, who lived in the same city as them. But I knew my pictures were upstairs in Ha-momma room on her dresser. Why I don't know but I think about it now and she didn't even deserve to have a picture of me at all. I remember going in the living room and dining room and looking at all the pictures of my cousins and not one of me anywhere. When my daddy wasn't around my mommy would always tell me that they did not like us. Why I never knew why.

On Christmas my gift from my Ha-momma would be some ugly sweater from the D&K dollar store or a pair of socks. She would give my mother some dish towels or some underwear and my dad some socks from the D&K dollar store. We never got gifts from my daddy sister but I would always buy her one and Ha-momma one from the Christmas gift sale at school. I would see my cousins open there gifts up and they would be in JCPenny's boxes my gift wasn't even wrapped she would leave it in the bag it came in. That is how I know it came from the D&K store. I never got a birthday gift or a birthday card from my Ha-momma or her daughter. But my big momma and my two Uncles that lived in the same city as I did always gave me something. They would always give me money and my mommy would take me to store and let me buy whatever I wanted with my money.

My Big momma would send me food stamps every month. I couldn't wait to get my envelope in the mail from her. I would be so excited she loved me like a grandmother should and she treated us all the same.

My one Uncle that lived above a store downtown and he worked there also. Every Sunday my mommy would take him dinner for the week and he would in return give us boxes of can goods from the store. He always had a box of candy for me all kinds of candy bars. One time he gave me a radio but I couldn't take it in the house. My Uncle had pets called little roaches but I didn't mind when I went to his house everyone isn't perfect plus he treated me like family. So my dad took me outside to unscrew the little yellow radio and I did. To may surprise 1000 roaches ran out of it. I was too scared to touch the radio again and my daddy threw it in the garbage. I didn't want to hurt my Uncle feeling so whenever he asked me about the radio I lied and told him I loved it and it was working just fine. Sometimes it was the thought that counted. His kindness made me not judge my father's family but their actions towards me made me judge them.

My Uncle that lived downtown he was a loner. He never came to our house for a visit. My mom and I would always go see him on Sunday like clockwork. Sometimes my dad and my other uncle would go by his house after they went fishing to show him what they caught or to give him so fish. I didn't know anything about him. I don't think he ever had any children. My father would always say that my uncle was the fighter of the group he liked to carry a razor to cut people. And my dad and my uncle would sit and tell stories about him and all the fights he got into. So he was the bad boy of the group. Why he stayed so distant from the rest of the family I never knew. But I did know that he loved me and cared about me. Every Sunday was Christmas when I seen him. Even thou I was just going to get some candy from him I couldn't wait to get that.

My father's mother had 6 children. My father was the oldest, then my uncle that smelled like pee pee was the second. He and my dad looked just like twins. Then my other uncle who lived downtown was the third child. Then my aunt who lived in New York City was the fourth and then my aunt who lived in the same city with me and last my other uncle who lived down south. All of the siblings looked exactly alike except for my one uncle. He was average height, very skinny and dark skinned. My mommy said he had a bad grade of hair that is why his head was always bald. He did not resemble any of the other siblings not even his own mother. And the picture I have of my grandfather he didn't resemble him either. Why he did for a living I never exactly knew. My daddy was an automatic and my one uncle was a roofer. My aunt that lived in the same city as us she worked at a factory and her sister was in the health field and the youngest he was in the ministry. But I never knew what my other uncle did for a living. He didn't own a car he always caught public transportation to get to and from or he rode his bike all over town. My mommy would joke and say that he was a hussler what he hussled I don't know. But his apartment was very clean nothing was out of place. He was very picky about things if you moved a pillow on his couch he would get upset. So the rule was to never touch anything when you went to visit him. And take whatever items he gave you with a smile. One time he was giving us some items that he had taken from the grocery store below where he worked. And I complained and said I didn't want something. I think it was some 3 Musketeers candy bars. I did not like that kind my favorite were Almond Joy or a Snickers bar. And I was asking him to please get me some of those instead in the voice of an 8 year old child. My uncle instantly got mad and started complaining and for the next 2 or 3 weeks he would not open the door for us when we went to go take him his Sunday dinner. We had to leave it at the door. My mother said it was because I had something. Then she told me to never complain when someone gives you something just take it with a smile you never know when they might give you something you really need one day.

But my uncle was like that. If my mommy fixed him something that he did not like instead of saying he didn't like he would get mad and not open the door the following Sunday. Maybe he had some mental illness or disorder and at the time there was no name for it and since family knew how he was we just accepted it. No one wanted to upset him. I know my mother didn't that was her free weekly groceries and my free weekly candy.

I can still picture him standing in front of the store on the corner with his hat on. He always dressed well. Nice shiny shoes and a long sleeve button up sweater and dress pants and button up shirt. I never saw him wear jeans or sneakers. He was always dressed in business attire if you passed him on the street you would assume he worked at an office. But in reality I don't think he had more than a third grade education. The one thing I will always remember and love about him is that he was a smooth dresser at all times and during all seasons. Shoes always shiny and the hat had to match the shoes. I loved him so much I named one of the sons after him later on.

My Uncle that lived downtown passed away when I was around 13. He couldn't read very well and they think he may have over dosed on his medication that he was taking at the time. We couldn't have an open casket funeral because he had been dead for a couple of days before his body was found. It was the second funeral I had ever been to. It was a small funeral no more than 15 people there wasn't any singing or preaching no one hanging on to the casket. We were all dressed in black I remember seeing my father's mother crying it was the first time I had seen her in 5 years. I didn't even think she had heart that could cry. Death has a way of bringing people together even if for a quick minute. I remember us at my Ha-momma house after the funeral my Uncle's girlfriend at the time was there also. I don't know exactly what happened or what tick my father off that day. Maybe he had too many drinks and with the unexpected death of his brother was too much. My father and his first two brothers were very close and they each were different. There past glued them together. The things they went through back in the early 1900's and the stories they shared about growing up glued them together. The first set of 3 kids had a different child hood from the second set of 3 kids. But I know my father blew up about something and I remember him saying "that is why you had daddy killed to marry his brother you knew he wasn't daddy son" to my grandmother. After he said that you know they put us out the house. But the story that my father and my Uncle use to talk about was that Ha-momma was messing around with her husband's brother. They never called him by name they always referred to him as "daddy's brother". And that my grandfather found out about it and confronted his brother and her. And that was when the brother of my grandfather along with some friends killed him in an alley and then married my grandmother which was his sister-n-law. And that my deceased Uncle was not my grandfather son but his brother's son. And yes my Uncle did not look like anybody in the family he stood out like a sore thumb. My other Uncle also agreed with the story I heard it many times from them when they would sit around and drink and talk about the old days. But they always agreed on this one particular story.

When my father use to talk about use to talk about my grandfather his face would light up like a little kid. He would tell me that my grandfather was a mean man he didn't play. If he told you to do something he didn't ask twice. And that he loved to hunt. I have a picture of him with his hunting dogs. You can tell by the picture he was living a hard life. How old was he in the picture I don't know. You can tell in his picture that he had large hands and big feet and that he was serious person. My father told me on the day that he was killed that his father's spirit came to the house a few times. "I remember that night. His dogs were barking loud and they never barked. My father had trained them to be quiet unless they were out hunting. I ran outside and I seen his dogs barking and standing on the fence like someone was standing there with them. But I didn't see anything. We went back to bed and when I went to sleep I woke up again because the dogs were barking and when I looked out I seen my daddy standing at the gate so I went back to bed. But in the morning they told me he had been killed in an alley. And I knew in my heart what had happened to him. He was murdered. My father was strong man he was a fighter everyone in town was scared of him. But for about 3 nights his spirit came to the house and you would see him standing by the fence by his dogs. He loved his dogs". Sometimes he would cry when he talked about his father. My uncle and my father would share their memories of him and I knew they loved him deeply. Maybe they were upset about how his death came about. Fifty years later and counting they were still shedding tears for their murdered father. After his death they relocated from the south to Detroit.

My dad was so mad that his father was gone and how he was murdered and why he was murdered. He held a grudge against his mother for it up until the day she died. Even thou he loved her and respected her as his mother he had a grudge against her for the death of his father. And I think after that incident at the house my father side of the family cut us off completely. We had no contact with his other sister or her kids or anyone else in his family. Everyone had the same last name except for my Grandmother. I never saw any pictures of her when she was younger or of my grandfather or of her last husband. If she did have pictures she never shared them with me. All I see now is a 300 pound plus white looking woman in front of me. Maybe she was something to kill for back in the day I don't know. She never had any kids with her second husband. I know that my father did have other family member living in the city. I don't if they were from his mother side or his father side. They lived in the Humboldt park area but I never met them I just knew they lived in the area. When I was in high school I had two teachers approach me and ask who my parents were and asked who my grandparents were and I told them and they replied that we were related that they were my cousins. I told my father but he just shrugs it off. They lived in that area many years ago so it could have been true. My even knew my grandmothers name and her daughter and their address. But why we never mingled with them I don't know. I asked my mother did my father have relatives on that side of town and she said yes. She said that she only met a few of them one time back when she first met my father. But hasn't heard or seen them since. She said she didn't know why they didn't mingle with my grandmother and her daughter. Her excuse was that "You know your daddy people are funny acting people no one can get along with them for too long".

But my Big Momma would send me something a million miles away just for me. My Big Momma always made me feel special even when I was around all my cousins she always made each of us feel special. My Big Momma use to get food stamps back when they were colored dollar bills. And every month she would send me a letter and it would have some food stamps in it. Not only did she do it for me but she did it for each of her grandchildren. She never made a difference between us. But when it came to my father's mother I was lucky if I got a hello from her.

My father sister always had a way of acting like I didn't exist. I had some cousins which were some of her grandchildren that would be over there sometimes when I was there. One was a girl she was the same age as I and a lot shorter than me and I'm short enough. She had very long hair longer than mine. She always acted stuck up I think she was born stuck up. Her father is my first cousin he had her when he around 16 by a woman who was a lot older than him. He went on and had two daughters by a woman that lived around the corner from them one was light skinned like her mother and I never had a problem with her. But the other was short, fat, dark and ugly. She had snotty ways like the people on my father's side of the family had. Her nose was always up in the air like her half older sister was always turned up in the air.

My father sister would wear a lot of make-up it would take her up to an hour to put it all on her face. Sometimes when I was over there she would be getting ready for work and when her oldest granddaughter was there we would go in her room and watch her put on a hundred pounds of makeup. If the granddaughter wasn't there I didn't go around her too much. My mommy and daddy said she looked like a clown every time they seen her with that shit all over her face. And she would wear those long fake finger nails and eyelashes. She did all of this makeup work to go work in a factory. It wasn't like this is Sunday like for church she did this everyday she would not leave the house unless she had on hundred pounds of makeup. Her oldest grand daughter was just like her. Since I could remember she always wore a ton of makeup on her face and at nine years old she had more makeup than Avon. My Aunt would give her purses and fill it up with all her old makeup. My daddy said I couldn't wear that "shit" he didn't like it and didn't want me to get in the habit of putting it on. To this day I don't wear makeup lipstick is as far as I go.

I would watch my Aunt cook food for her granddaughters, herself and her boyfriend. Not once did she ever offer me a crumb of bread off the floor. They would drink juice and soda while I had to drink water from the sink. Whenever I asked Ha-momma for something she would say that's "theirs" or that's "not mine" or that's "just for them" don't touch it. The only time I got something was if it was Ha-momma food that she brought or a pie or cake that Ha-momma made and no one else wanted to eat it. I couldn't even get a glass of juice or soda not even a cookie when I was over there unless I brought my on food. Who ever heard of bringing your own food to your grandmother and aunt house to eat? I never understood what they had against me. She was my Aunt but she treated me like a stranger or like I made her stomach turn whenever she looked at me. I always brought her gifts on Christmas and cards for her birthday because I was young and was being taught to love your family. Not once did I ever receive a gift from her not even a hug not even a thank you or I like the gift you gave me. It's a shame my mommy had to pack me a lunch whenever I went over to visit my family. If she didn't I wouldn't eat. They wouldn't feed me not because they didn't have the food but because they were taking some sort of bullshit out on me. I promise myself I would never treat my grandchildren like that. Even if I was mad at my children or their spouse I would never take it out on my grandchildren. I know how bad it hurt me and I would not want to hurt them. When you think of Grandparents you think of some sort of humanly angel. That is what I thought my big momma was an angel. But when it came to my father's mother she was the devil himself.

But you don't have to always speak with your tongue to let someone know that you don't like them. Your actions do it for you a matter of fact actions are better than words. Actions are sometimes the truth. You can lie with your tongue but that body language and action will tell the truth every time. My father sisters didn't have to say they didn't like me they showed it. Ha-momma didn't have to tell me she tolerated me she showed it. My daddy's other Aunt and his other sister and her kids didn't have to say they didn't like us they showed it. And my cousins who were the same age as me didn't have to speak it whatever shit was packed up my daddy's side of the family ass was also packed up their offspring ass too. Even my Aunt and her kids and my other Auntie who lived hundreds of miles away had a problem with me and my mother. They would come and visit my father's mother and his sister and they wouldn't tell us they were in town sometimes my daddy would just show up for a visit and they would be there. They wouldn't even speak it was like they looked straight through us. I was a child and I couldn't understand it but actions always spoke louder than words.

I remember Ha-momma telling me I had a sister a lot older than me back in Detroit but I forgot her name and that I had a brother I think they were born when my dad was 18 but I never asked my daddy about this. She asks me did I know about this I told her no. Maybe this is the reason they didn't like me. I am not for sure. I just know I was tolerated while I was in there presence. Why she told me this I don't know but my daddy never mention them to me when I was younger. But as I got older my mother said did you know when your dad was 18 he was already out there making babies. But they never showed me any pictures of them or if they had contact with them. My dad never talked about them. I don't know if it was because they had a terrible break up or a bad marriage. I know that he was married before to whom I don't know. If he had children out of this marriage I don't know. My father never spoke of it. I guess he was trying to bury it.

I remember one day I was over at my grandmother house. Because no one at home to watch me. And while I was watching my Aunt as usual make lunch for my boyfriend and her granddaughter and herself. As usual she was mixing up the hamburger meat with chopped onions and bell peppers. He always had to have homemade hamburgers every single day before he went to work. She and her granddaughter were talking about something and her boyfriend was at the kitchen table reading the newspaper. He had a big nasty mole on his face next to his nose just a little above his lip. It looked almost like a small golf ball I swear if I grabbed it I could pull it off his face. He was light skinned like my dad wore glasses all the time he was medium built and always rode a motorcycle. He worked at one of the auto factories in the city. But on this particular day I was hungry I think I forgot my bag of goodies at home and I didn't have any money today to walk to the store up the street. I only had maybe 90 minutes to wait and my mother would have been there to get me. But those hamburgers where smelling good. My Aunt makes one for her boyfriend, her granddaughter and herself and she proceeds to put the rest of the hamburger meat mixture back into the refrigerator. I tell my Aunt I am hungry and may I have a burger like them. Well to my surprise they all ignored me and continued to eat and talk among themselves. Ha-momma yells from the sitting room what is wrong and I tell her "I want a hamburger." She tells me "Your momma will be here in a little while you can eat when you get home". I tell my Aunt again I wanted a hamburger like them. Ha-momma tells me again "You're not getting a hamburger so come in here with me and sit down".

Like I said I couldn't have been no older than 8. I was just learning how to talk but I knew how to cuss. I heard it all the time my mommy, my daddy and my uncle were pro's at it. I have imitated them long enough that I could cuss the best curser in the world out with my eyes closed and my hands tied behind my back. I don't remember exactly what it was that I had said back to her but I remember telling her I was "sick of this shit" and "I am never coming over here again". And then Ha-momma told me to "Take your ass on and don't come back over here anymore". It wasn't a problem for me I had my house key tied on a string around my neck. I walked out the house and off the porch and started my journey home. I had driven in the car plenty of times to my Ha-momma house. I didn't know the names of the streets I was on. But I knew the way to go to get back home. I remember certain houses and building so I just walked. It seemed like forever to get home but I made it there. Later on my mommy came home and I told her what happened and that I was never going back over there again. And I didn't for a very long time. On days when I didn't have school I was allowed to stay home alone. My mommy would call and check on me and sometimes my daddy would come home on his lunch break to check on me. One time my daddy came home for his lunch break to check on me and he fell asleep on the couch. I was bored so I got out my hair ribbons and makeup. While my father slept I but all type of ribbons in his hair and painted his face with makeup. I even painted his finger nail with red polish. He jumped up and asked what time it was and I said it 3 o'clock. He said "dam I am late". He ran to the bathroom and that is when he noticed that he had on makeup. He screamed "what the hell did you do girl". I started laughing even thou he was mad he started laughing as well. He hurried up and washed off the makeup. I had put ribbons in his hair but before he went into the bathroom he grabbed his hat and placed it on his head. When my daddy made it back to work he took off his hat and his co-workers noticed all the pretty ribbons he had in his hair and the nice red polish he was wearing. They teased him for the rest of the day. He called me when finally seen all that I have done to him. "I am going to kill you when I get home" he said then we both busted out laughing and he hung up the phone. I don't know why my brother couldn't watch me this summer. I think maybe he had gone down south that summer without us I don't know. But I do know 5 years would past before I went back over to Ha-momma house again. I think when I graduated the 8th grade that I went over there again.

I am getting older now becoming a teenager. I have one big tit and one small tit. But my momma told me not worry because they will grow and be the same size in a little while. She said sometimes one get big and the other one catches up to it later on. Of course she didn't take me to the doctor that would be too much like right. She called her sister and whatever her sister tells her then it must be right! So now I will have big tits like the other girls on my street. And I will start to look like the girls in the magazines and be able to wear high heel shoes.

My butt is getting bigger my mom and dad keeps teasing me about it. They say I have a butt just like my Great Aunt down south. She is the only female family member that has a booty so I must have gotten it from her. I'm getting taller but I'm not as tall as the other kids on my street. They all say I am short. My momma says I took after my dad and will be short like him. The people on my mother side of the family and fairly tall people.

I have a friend. She is my neighbor's grand-daughter. She has two brothers. One has a funny eye he isn't cute to me at all or any other girl on the street. The other one is alright looking he is short like me but he has big rabbit teeth. She tells me that he what's me to be his girlfriend. She is one year younger than me but she is a lot smaller than me. She looks like a little kid but she is almost a teenager but can pass for a third grader. Me and her youngest brother I are the same age.

Whenever my friend comes over to her grandmother house we always play together upstairs in my bedroom or downstairs in her grandmother basement. She is the only friend of mine that my mother lets come into the house and play with me. I think because my parents are good friends with her grandparents. It's always me and her alone in my room. My mom said I can only have one friend at a time in the house. Sometimes we play house together. She is the mom and I am the dad. Or sometimes I am the mom and she is the dad. When I am the dad I lay on top of her because I am a boy and boys lay on top of girls. My brother lays on top of me. She doesn't tell me to stop even when I rub up and down on her like my brothers does me. I even put my fingers between her legs like my brothers does me and she doesn't say anything. She lays there like I do when my brother is on top of me. And when she plays the dad she does the same thing to me. We kiss each other on the mouth. I touch her titties and she touch mine and we even kiss each other between the legs. This went on between us until we became teenagers. To us during this time none of this is wrong. We use to laugh and say "this is grownups" do and since we are acting like we are grownups then it is okay.

Back then it was normal for us to touch each other in that way. But now that I replay these things in my head what was she going through.

We acted out everything that was done to us. Was one of her brothers touching her like that? She was the only friend that I had that I did this with. I had other girls that I played with but we never did anything like me and her. Whenever we played we always had imaginary boyfriends. This way it is so important to pay close attention to your children when they play. Watch how they play with dolls or other kids. Listen to the words they use when they play especially alone. They will always repeat what they hear or act out what has happened to them. My parents didn't pay attention. My father was busy drinking and my mother was busy trying to keep the peace so my father didn't act a fool.

I had other friends that came over but when we played we always played as sisters or mothers and daughters. No one was a boy or a daddy except when I was with her. And I felt safe to touch her and I let her touch me. Sometimes we would just lay on the floor and hug each other. Finding comfort with a person who shared your secret pain that you or she had no words for.

I learned that the thing between a boy legs was called a dick. And that all boys have one even my dad, my brother and uncle. And that the thing between a girls leg is called a pussy. All girls have one and babies come out of them when you get big and have a husband or a boyfriend. My momma has never told me this. My friend she taught me that when girls and boys are naked the dick goes inside the pussy. We didn't know how it goes in there it just go in there. She said she didn't know why she just said that is how it goes. So when we played we would practice on one another using our fingers. She even taught me how to kiss with a tongue. We would practice sometimes when we were in my room playing. Since I was her brother girlfriend I had to kiss him because that is what girlfriends and boyfriends did together. When I did sneak and kiss him every now and then she would stand there and watch and laugh and say I didn't do it right or her brother didn't do it right. Where she learned this from I don't know and I never asked her. At this time of my life there were still movies that I couldn't watch. If my father thought a grown up scene was coming on he would tell me to go in the kitchen or he would cover my eyes until it was over.

Well my momma never told me any of this stuff. And my friend told me not to tell her because she would get in trouble. So I kept her little secrets to myself. I didn't even share them with my other friends on the street. She wasn't friends with them and didn't really play with them when she came over to visit her grandparents.

So when my brother lays on top of me does that mean I'm his girlfriend? According to my friend that is what boyfriends and girlfriends did. But her brother and I never did that we just kissed. And years down the road her brother grew up to be a rapist and killer.

I'm getting older now. My dad says I can wear fingernail polish and lip gloss. Sometimes I put Vaseline on my lips. I like the way the Vaseline makes them shine. I have tits now but not as big as the women on television but I have some that are kind of small but at least I need a training bra.

We go fishing a lot we have been going fishing for as long as I can remember. My dad loves to fish. To some people that is his nick name Fish. None of my other friends go fishing with their family like I do. I, my dad, my momma, and sometimes my Uncle go fishing together. Sometimes my brother goes with us but not all the time. We go to Lewiston and fish down the hill behind the Art Park Museum right on the Niagara River. It's pretty I can see the rainbow bridge it's just a 100 feet away. I can see Canada across the river and sometimes on a clear day I can see the mist from Niagara Falls. I'm not good at fishing but I just enjoy going. But they let me take the fish off the hook when they catch them. I never learned how to swim my parents can't even swim. But I wade out in the water. I go until the water reaches my waist. But if the current is too swift I stay closer to land and only go until it reaches my knees. Sometimes I can see fish swim in front of me. And sometimes when the bait gets low I look under rocks in the water and I catch small crawfish for them to use as bait. I don't mind doing that I just want to stay in the calmness of the river for as long as I can. To me this is sanctuary.

I have a half sister she is older than me and we have different mommas. I guess my dad cheated on my momma and made her with is other girlfriend that would explain why my mother hates my half sister so much. But come to find out that my mother and my half sister mother were friends once upon a time. And he was dating my mother and messing with the friend also. He wanted to marry my half sister mother but she refused to marry him because she knew what type of man he was a control freak and drunk and he wanted a slave not a wife. My father had a history of drinking and being violent when he did drink. Everyone that knew my father knew that. When he would drink everyone would always make sure he was happy they made sure to not upset him in any type of way. Well he ended up marrying my mother I guess she was easier to mold into what it was that he wanted. She was stuck in a city far away from home she had nowhere to go so she had no choice but to take his shit and make the best of it. So my half sister mother ended up getting pregnant during the time he was married to my mother I guess she didn't want to marry him but didn't mind to continue sleeping with him even after he had gotten married to my mother.

All my half sister does is complain when she is over at the house. Why do you have this why do you have that. I never get anything. I need new shoes I need new clothes. She didn't like me she said I was spoiled rotten because I had so much stuff but the stuff I had was once someone else's stuff. My mother and I went to different Thrift stores and I would get a lot of stuff because it was cheap. My momma told me not to tell anyone and once you put it on no one knows where you got it from. The only time I got something new was on Christmas and a few items for the first day of school to wear. For the other days of the year I wore whatever I could get from the thrift stores. Every Saturday rain or shine we would go but if the weather was nice we would go garage sale shopping in the white neighborhoods.

I remember when I was smaller than I am now maybe around six years old my dad took me to my sister's apartment. They lived on the West side of town near the Peace Bridge. My half sister mother was dying. I don't know why she was dying but we went to see her. She was laying in their front room on a hospital bed the lights were off. My dad held my hand and we walked into the room when we got next to the bed he told me to leave the room and go outside. But I sat in the other room in a chair I was able to watch him and her talk even thou I couldn't hear what they were saying to one another. I watch him sit in a chair next to her he took off his cap and held her hand. I never knew what he said to her I never asked and I never told my mommy about the visit. When my half sister mother died she was so upset. She had long hair like mine down her back and she took some scissor and cut all her hair off. My dad was so mad that she cut her hair. He loved long hair. She told me she did it because she was mad that her mother died. And that she looked in the mirror and started cutting her hair because she didn't know what else to do. I don't know what she saw when she looked in the mirror. She had to go live with her grandmother after the death of her mother and her other siblings that were older moved to Virginia I think. My mother wouldn't allow her to come live with use even thou she was my father daughter. When her mother died my sister visits were not as regular as they use to be. She told me that our father had promised her mother that she would be able to live with us after she died. And my half sister was very upset that he did not keep his promise and she blamed my mother for it. My father never gave her any support of any kind once her mother died.

But she came over sometimes after her mother died. I thought that she would come over more since her mother died but she didn't. I would see her maybe 2 times a year and we lived about 20 minutes from each other. And my mother would just look her up and down and sit on the couch pretending to be reading a book and just roll her eyes at her every time she said something. I never understood this it wasn't her fault she was born why not be mad at daddy? She complained every time she knew my half sister was coming over and my half sister would complain to me about her. But my daddy never said anything. My sister tells me she know my mother don't like her and my mother complain about how my sister doesn't appreciate anything. My mother would be buy her things from the thrift store and my half sister would refuse them so my mother said she was ungrateful. I have no memory of anything being brought for her for any reason. No Christmas gift, no school clothing no birthday gift. And sometimes my daddy and I would drive by her grandmother house and he would drop off money I don't know how much was given. Sometimes my half sister would come over and he would give her a few dollars if she would complain that is wasn't enough my mother would go off and start preaching about ungrateful she was. I was caught in the middle I couldn't take sides because I loved my mother and I loved my half sister even thou she didn't love me. Once she finished high school and became grown that was the end of our relationship. She had a daughter around the time my parents adopted my sister and was upset because my parents gave her my adopted sister old items. She felt that since she had the first biological grandchild of my father that she should get all this new stuff but it didn't work out that way and jealously took over. My father would go over there with my mother to go see my half sister and would take my niece used toys and my half sister would go off. Then one day my mother told my father that they were not going over there anymore because she was to ungrateful. My half sister and I got back in contact with each other around the time her daughter was 5 or 6 but it didn't work. That jealously or pain that she had hid inside her heart prevented us from having a relationship as sisters. Things that my father should have worked out with her he didn't and I was trying to have a relationship with her and that caused issues between me and my mother. My sister said she would call the house and our dad would tell her that she could not come over because my mother had now retired and was home all the time. Why my daddy allowed my mother to cut off communication between him and his child I will never know. But just like she was trapped to stay with him and accept his ways he was now trapped. He is not the young man he use to be. He is twenty years older than my mother his health isn't that great and she is holding the reins that he use to hold against her. Karma is a bitch.

I haven't seen my half sister in 20 years. I have not seen her other 2 children and she has not seen of my last 3 children. Maybe if she had a better relationship with my dad things would have been better between us. We just never sat down and talked to one another. When we did it was daddy make me sick or your mother gets on my nerves. I didn't want to hear or talk about something I couldn't control I just wanted to establish a sister to sister relationship. One where I could be like "hey chick what's up you want to hang out" or "you want to take my kids and your kids to the park". Or be together for the holidays sometimes we never celebrated anything together.

We always go down south every year sometimes two or three times a year. My dad drives most of the way. My mother doesn't drive much she is afraid of bridges. One time she was driving while my dad was sleeping and she slammed on the brakes in the middle of the highway because she had come across a bridge that she needed to cross. My dad jumped up and started saying what the hell is going on "and she said "a bridge a bridge I can't drive across that". He was so mad because she had back up traffic and he had to get out and drive 1 minute across a bridge. Whenever we drove across bridges she would always duck down in her seat so she couldn't see the water or close her eyes and asked me to tell her when we made it over. But when we travel I mainly sleep all the way. I couldn't drive but I could read the road signs to tell my dad how far we have to go to the next city. And I always keep an eye on the gas gauge I am not trying to walk.

My Big Momma has a new house built and we are all excited to see it. The house she had before was a literally a shack but everyone enjoy going there and everyone was happy when we were together like a family. She had a way of making everyone feel loved and happy when they are around her. She cooked and cooked and all my aunts and my mother would cook and we ate all the time when we were there. The music would be playing and all the men would be out front playing cards and drinking and laughing. It was a happy feeling unlike the feeling I got when I was around by daddy's people. We never celebrated anything with my father's family. Never ate with them on the holidays and they lived less than 5 minutes away. And we have to travel 1500 miles to have a good time with family.

I wish I knew why my father's side of the family hated my mother and me so much. I know sometimes there is maybe one family member who doesn't like you. But my father's entire family hates my mother and me. His two brothers seemed to love me and mother to death but the other's could kill us with a look if they could. Then their children hate my mother and then their children's children hate my mother. And then they have distaste for me also because I'm her daughter. No one had ever spilled the beans on why she was hated so much. I guess that is one secret that will go to the grave with them all. My father never explained it to me. No matter what I tell him about the treatment I receive from his family he just ignores it. When he goes fishing he takes fish over there. When he grows his vegetable in the garden he is taking bags of fresh vegetables over there. He just totally ignores that fact about their treatment of me. I never understood it. Maybe he was hoping that by him giving those things it would make them treat me descent but it never happened. When I told him when I was 8 that I was never going back over there I meant that. He never had them say sorry to me. And when he would try and drive over there when I was in the car with them. I refused to get out of the car. I would sit in the car and look straight ahead until he got back in and we left. I was stubborn so when he would ask me "are you getting out" I would reply "no" and I stood my ground. I refuse to say sorry when I was the one getting unfair treatment. They would rather give a hungry dog a hamburger before me. Love and respect cannot be brought.

There was my Granny who was very old she was in a wheelchair during my memory of her that is who I am named after. Everyone loved Granny even the white town people. They all respected her decision and advice and everyone seemed to stay in harmony around her. She had been alive since the 1880's. She had stories of slavery and how many people came to her white and black to be healed by her medicines. She was 100% Indian and she knew the remedies of her parents and grandparents to heal different aliments. She was even a mid-wife to white folks back in the day when she was able to walk she help deliver almost half of the town residents at that time. She was 102 when she peacefully passed in her sleep one day. But me being a child I thought well she is in a wheelchair she can't do anything to me. I was at her house playing one day and I was catching frogs. Now she had already told me not to bring the frogs in the house. But me being hard headed decided to put the small frogs in my pocket. She called me in the house and told it was time for me to take a nap. So I climb up in her bed with a pocket full of small frogs. I remember her sitting in her wheelchair getting her hair done by my uncle wife my Aunt. She had long silver looking hair and would wear it in 4 plaints. It was silky like my father's hair. Then all of sudden I woke up to screaming. The small frogs had gotten out of my pocket and were jumping around the room. I jumped up she said "didn't I tell you not to bring those frogs in the house get them out". I gathered all the small frogs and threw them out the door. But it didn't end there she told me to come over to her chair. My Aunt grabbed me and held me in place and I got my ass tore up by Granny. I ran on the porch and told her "I was going to my Big momma" she told me "go on then with your hard headed tail". It didn't end there when I made it down the long road to my Big Momma house I got another ass whipping from my mother for leaving Granny house and walking alone on the dirt road. They lived on a highway so big trucks were always speeding down the road so it would be hard for them to see a little six year old walking in the road. Or by the time they seen it would be too late and I would hit and killed. But that day just wasn't my day. But I learned if your elder is still breathing, talking and in their right mind and you do wrong you will get your ass tore up.

I remember when my Granny died I can still see the funeral in my head as clear as day. We jumped in the truck and my dad drove all the way there nonstop my mom was crying all the way there. This was my first funeral and I didn't understand when they said someone was dead. I was only six so I had not comprehended what death was. For her funeral I wore a light blue dress trimmed with little flowers. I couldn't really hear what the preacher was saying at the funeral all the small kids were seated at the back of the church. I just remember looking around and being amazed by all the people that were there. It was so many people at the church that some had to stand outside the church. There were black and white people a lot of them I had never seen before they were all crying over Granny death. I was too young to cry I didn't really understand what death met at the time what it really meant to lose someone. And this was the first funeral I had ever been to and I really didn't know what a funeral was or what it met. I remember when they were carrying Granny casket out of the church and my Big Momma was holding on to the casket screaming and crying and they had to pull her off of the casket. In private I imitated how Big Momma was acting when I was with my cousins. We laughed about it because we thought it was funny we didn't understand what had happened to our Granny or why our Big Momma felt that way. This was the first time we had ever seen our parents act this way. Granny was the backbone of our family she held it together until the end. She kept family members respectful to one another and when she past the family fell apart. The entire family was against one another. Granny had 5 children with my great grandfather but he had other children by his first wife. I am really not sure but when Granny died each of her children with their children all turned against one another. Cousins and Aunts that I use to be around I could no longer be around. I couldn't go to their house anymore. When she past the whole family just went up in strive. I never knew why or understood why. I was too young to understand the talks that were going on around me. My Big momma sister was one of her neighbors and after the death of Granny they became bitter enemies. We no longer played with my cousins or talked to them. Overnight love turned into over night hate. My mother would tell me they were all full of hate and evil people. And that they were going to pay for being that way. Each side felt they were right and was justified in hating the other. I know the war between them all had something to do with the church. The family owned this long stretch of land each sibling had a plot of the land and built a home on it and in the middle was the church. A very small church but it had been the family church for decades. My mother said that the one sister who was the oldest closed the church down and that started the war that would continue to go on throughout the family with no end. But this year for the first time I paid attention to what my cousins call my brother. They call him "Uncle". That means he is my uncle and not my brother he is my mother's brother.

My mother had one of her first cousins come live with us when I was younger. He worked at a car factory as well. That was the money making jobs in the city automobile factory work. My cousin was tall with dark skin and had a funny sounding voice. He has a son down south that lives with his mother. We are close in age. I play with him every time I go see my big momma. His grandmother is my big momma sister and they are neighbors. He lived with us when we lived on Northland. My parents started asking him for rent money and he got upset. He felt that since he was family he should be able to stay their rent free even if he did have a full time factory job. He moved out and I may have seen him 2 or 3 times after that. His son mother dies when he was young maybe around the age of 7. I remember it because it was close after the time Granny had died. Well no one was able to reach him to tell him she had died. And his mother was now taking care of his son and she wanted him to come there to get his son. So my mother decided to go to his house. We went a couple of times she would say he was there but just wouldn't let us in. Then one day he finally opened the door and we went inside his house. The outside of the house looked like a beat down shack but when you went inside it was a different story. Everything in the house was all white. He had white furniture, carpet, blinds and white curtains. We stood at the front door and all I saw was white. He and my mother talked and she was explaining to him that his mother down south was trying to call him to tell him to come get his son since his mother had died. After the conversation we got in the car and my mother was complaining about him. "Did you see his house? He is a god dam fagit" she said. "What mother fucker you know has an all white house"? She said. I didn't know what to say. My father came home from work and my mother started complaining about her cousin and how the conversation went. "I wish he would take that boy. He can afford to take care of him. He shouldn't leave him down there" she screamed while talking to my father. Well he never went to go get his son. He left him down there for his mother to raise she was already in her late 60's. My mother bitched about that for a long time. We would run into him when we were at the bank or the grocery store and he would not even speak to us. I remember one time seeing him at the bank when I with my mother. He had on a bunch of gold chains and rings. He was also wearing a floor length mink coat. He looked over at us and my mother says "If you can dress like that you can take care of your dam son". He looked us up and down and walked out the bank. In my mind he was the best dresser I have ever seen and his house was laid. Whatever a fagit was at the time in my life I wanted to be one. If I could be laced in gold chains and mink coats and driving a trans-am car I will be one. But that was my first portrait of a dead beat dad. When AIDS first came out it was labeled a homosexual disease she use to always wish that him. Why was she so crossed with him I never understood it. I never understood a lot of my mother actions this is just one of many.

My uncle is getting bigger almost a grown man and I am getting bigger also. Both of my tits are finally the same size. I am finally wearing a bra which I thought I would like to wear but now that I am wearing one this dam thing gets on my nerves. I am always getting in trouble because I am always running around with the dam thing off.

Some kids get mad at me because I am the only child. They always say you get "everything you want". But I really don't. I just have a lot of stuff. Me and my momma go out early in the morning on Saturdays when she doesn't have to work and go to Saint Vincent DePaul thrift store. It's around the corner from our house on Genesee Street and Colorado. We get a lot of used clothes there and other things. We get so many clothes there for cheap that my mom sends boxes of clothes down south and she give clothes to my Uncles. My mom told me that "nobody knows where your clothes come from once you put them on". This must have been the only advice about life that she gave me that I remember and still use. She taught me how to use coupons and how coupons save you money when you buy groceries. I couldn't wait for the Sunday paper to come so I could cut out coupons and save us some money when we went grocery shopping. She taught me how to shop at thrift stores, look for clearance items at other stores and go to garage sales and look for markdown food at the grocery store. I am glad she shared this information with me at a young age but sooner than I think she won't be teaching me anything or sharing any information with me regarding. I become invisible to her and her looks towards me will remind me of how she use to look at my half sister.

So my friends seen that I had a lot of nice stuff. Whenever they asked where it came from I would say "my mom brought it" and that was that. It wasn't a lie she did buy it where it came from that was none of their business. When they tried to get me to say which store she got it from I will tell them "I don't know I came home from school and it was on my bed".

My uncle room door is open it doesn't have a lock on it. He has girlfriends now and I hate them all. In my mind at this point in my life I am his girlfriend he lays on top of me in his bed when no one else is there. So whenever he asks me to do something now I won't do it. I usually tell him "fuck you" or "no" he say some shit back but I don't care I am mad and I know how to cuss people out. He makes me sick in my mind he is cheating on me. I go through his dresser and I read the letters they write him. He tells my momma that I go through his stuff but who cares I still do it anyway he is my boyfriend in my mind. My momma tells me to stay out of his room stop going through his stuff. But when he and I look at each other he knows what is going on in my mind.

This particular summer I am getting on a plane. I have never been on a plane before. I am going down south but not too Big Momma house I am going to see my Aunt and my two cousins. I am going all by myself momma said the tickets cost too much so I have to be a big girl and go by myself. I am so excited I can't wait to see my cousin. We have the same name except I am #1 because I was born first. I am 109 days older than her. My momma complains about us having the same name she said she wish she never told her sister what she was naming me because she stole my name. But she won't dare tell her sister that.

My cousin and I are total opposites. My mom and her mom are sisters. They talk all the time for hours at a time. My mom has to tell her everything I mean everything. Even if she has to whisper it to her so my dad doesn't hear. They are very close the kind of relationship I wish I had with someone. The kind of relationship I wish I had with my half sister. No one on my mother's side of the family knows that my dad has other children. In their eyes I am the only child he has. My mother has been good at burying her existence. She made sure to remind me to not tell anyone that she does exist.

My Aunt has a new husband. I never saw him before. I think they just got married. He seems nice I have no reason not to like him. My cousins never said they didn't like him.

My Aunt has a nice house with a big back yard. It's a one story house like Big Momma we live in a two story house. But it hot down here you never see any children outside walking around and playing like up north.

I met my second boyfriend here. His name is Derrick. He reminds me of my dad. He is light skinned, kind of short and has some pretty jet black curly hair. He comes over when my Aunt and Uncle leave for work. We stand out in the carport for a few hours every day. We hug and kiss and talk about how we will be when we grow up and get married. My friend has already taught me how to kiss a few months ago. And when he rubs his dick up against me I don't get mad or scared because my uncle does it all the time to me at home. My little cousin always trying to blackmail me and tell me he is telling his mom when she gets home. At this time in life little kids can still be bribe with candy. And every day until I leave we watch the clock and at 2 he leaves and we rush in to do our chores.

My Aunt husband is nice to me he is cool. He is a tall man medium build. I don't know what he does for a living I think he does some kind of mechanic work his clothes always have that dark grease on them like my dad back home does. I know that he does not have any children. And by the conversation that my parents had back home he was mad that my Aunt could not have any children.

Then why would you marry her if she could not give you what you wanted.

Me and my Aunt husband always sit together and watch television. Sometimes I sit next to him and sometimes I sit between his legs. And sometimes I sit on his lap and I could feel his dick in his pants just like my uncle back at home. He doesn't touch me in any way but I can feel it. And maybe in his mind he doesn't know that I know what a dick is yet.

My cousin is so the opposite of me. We are definitely oil and water. The only thing we have in common is our names and that we are related by blood. I wouldn't dare tell her about me and my friend back home and what we talk about and what we do. She isn't like that and she may think I'm nasty or something. I don't even tell her I know about dicks or pussys or that I have seen our uncles dick. She might think I am to fast so I decide to keep all my secrets to myself. She is my favorite cousin and I never want her to stop talking to me. But we don't always get what we wish for. I think she is really the only person I talk to but not about everything because like I said we are total opposites.

Derrick is so sweet he brought me a silver ring. It has a white pearl and a black pearl mounted on it with 2 small diamonds. He promises to marry me one day. We even talk about kids. We are having 8 and he loves no one but me. Teenage love is what they call it. We promise to write each other until I come back next summer to see him again.

Unfortunately promises are met to be broken. I wrote him he never wrote back. I heard that Derrick got caught up in the drug game a few years later. Prison is now his big white house. He may have eight kids like he wanted but probably by multiple women. I replay our little summer romance in my head every now and then. He brought me so much joy that summer. That ring was the highlight of my life. That is also the reasons why I prefer pearls over diamonds.

I'm back home now from my summer vacation. I am starting to look like a little woman. My hair is black and long down my back which is unusual for a black girl to have. I always hear the question is that your real hair you must be mixed with something.

I wear a bra now all the time and I have pretty legs well that is what the boys say. I can wear fingernail polish. I have over 50 different bottles of polish and I make sure my polish matches what I wear so every night a new polish is put on. And I can wear lipstick now and for the next 20 years red lipstick will be my choice of color.

My uncle still lays on me but not a lot maybe every now and then. Sometimes he puts his fingers in my pussy and sometimes he puts his dick in my mouth. I still haven't figured out what's that stuff that be in my mouth when he done. And my friend she doesn't come over to her grandmother house that much anymore since her grandmother died. So I have no way of knowing and no one to ask.

And the friend that I do have they don't talk about anything like that.

I'm not sure exactly how old I am put it's around the age of 12 or 13 that I get introduced to what a dick feels like inside of me.

He had girlfriends his age all around him. Some would even come to house and be with him in his room with the door closed. Every teenage girl in our neighborhood wanted to be his girlfriend. He was very tall and nice looking finished high school and was in college. But what motivated him to always take advantage of me whenever he got the chance?

He was smart not to stick his whole dick inside of me. He put in just enough to get his enjoyment and after that he would shove his dick down my throat.

I never tried to fight him back not once. I never screamed. I never told anyone. I would just let him have his way. I think a part of me at this age knew it wasn't right but I just couldn't figure out how to tell anyone. I couldn't figure out how to say no. My mom worked second shift so I only seen her on the weekends if she wasn't working. My dad worked came home got drunk went to sleep. I wasn't close to any family that was near me I wasn't even close to my half sister. I couldn't run to my father's family for help they hated and never told me why. And I knew to not share anything with the girls in my neighborhood. They loved to gossip and there are a lot of he said she said fights all the time. So I know to just keep my thoughts and feeling buried.

The less people know the less they have to say that is what my dad always told me.

But not all of my childhood life was miserable. I had some fun memories here and there. I remember the first Wrestle Mania. I have always loved wrestling. My dad would get mad and change the channel "get that fake shit off my T.V" he would say whenever I would watch it. Back then we only had 1 television in the house and he was in control of that when he was home. But oh boy Wrestle Mania #1. My dad turned it to the pay preview channel and of course he wasn't about to pay for me to watch no "fake shit" even if I was his only daughter. So one of the boys on our street climbed up the utility pole did something to the cable box up there and a few houses on the block were able to watch Wrestle Mania for free. When it was over we ran outside talking about what happened and what we saw and what was the best match. But then we decided to re-enact what we saw and everyone wanted to re-enact Hulk Hogan. How would we do that? Easy we went a few doors down and a friend of mine pulled out some old mattresses his mother was throwing away and piled them up in the grass in the back yard. We all wanted to fly like Hulk Hogan so we all took turns jumping out of a second story window imitating how Hulk Hogan flew in the air in Wrestle Mania. What in the hell were we thinking about? What if we had missed the mattress and hit the concrete? I didn't care at that time I just wanted to practice my Hulk Hogan move. And one of the neighbors seen what we were doing and I got an ass whipping when I got home. When I got home my dad put some wrestling moves on my ass.

For some reason inside I was starting to hate this it has been routine for us to do this for as long as I could remember but a part of me had enough. My escape was now alcohol. My parents would make homemade wine in the basement every year. We would go to the market buy a bunch of concord grapes. Pick through the grapes even thou I got yelled at for eating so many of them. So drinking homemade wine was basically alcohol and it was nothing new to me. I have been helping my parents with wine making since I was a little girl. Picking the grapes ,adding the water, adding the sugar and straining it over and over again until it came out pulp free. My dad had a bar in the house where is kept his favorite alcohol drinks for himself and his friends when they came over. He loved to drink. So it was always in stock. He probably couldn't remember if he had drunk it or not. So whatever I drank wouldn't be missed. But when I knew I was going to be alone with my uncle sometimes in the middle of the night or when no one was around I would take me some drinks so I could sleep late. I knew once I woke up there was no way for me to avoid him if he was there. If I got up and left my room there was no way for me to say no to him. I did not have the strength or the courage to say no to him when he came time for him to lay with me. But if I stayed in my room asleep he couldn't ask me to come to his room. There could have been times when I was too drunk to know if he had touched me or not.

Whenever I took too much liquor I would just add water into the bottle and fill it back to where it was. Just like I use to do with the cough syrup. My dad would complain about the liquor being weak he never put it together that maybe someone was drinking I and replacing it with water. He would just complain that the companies are cheating him out of his money. And when I would go to the liquor store with him he would complain to the seller about it being weak. I had been going to the liquor with my father all my life so by the time I was 10 I knew exactly what he wanted. I could go in the liquor and pull the bottles off the shelf and place them on the counter for him while he stood in line and played is numbers. He always drank dark liquors the only white liquor he drank was good old fashion moonshine.

One day my uncle went too far. And I started to bleed afterwards. He had a strange look on his face. And I didn't know what to do. I went to the bathroom and got a bunch of tissues and small towels and put them up between my legs. I didn't tell my mom if she knew that my uncle hurt me she would be so mad at him and I don't want him to get in trouble. So I hid it. It was a long time before she found out about my bleeding. I don't know what happened to me mentally but around this time I started hating myself. My mind couldn't quite comprehend what exactly was going on with me but inside I hated it and every chance I got I tried to hurt myself or cause myself pain to myself.

One time I was in summer camp I had to be around 12 and we had a field trip to the YMCA in the white neighborhood to go swimming for the day. If you could not swim you had to stay in the shallow end of the pool which was only about 3 or 4 feet high if you could swim you could go in the deep end and jump off the diving board into the 10 feet pool of water. They had a floating barrier that separated the shallow end with the deep end of the pool. I knew I couldn't swim my parents never wanted me learn and they didn't feel it was important for me to learn. They didn't want to pay for the classes so that I could learn how to swim at the YMCA. I was upset that day and was tired of everything that was going on in my life. I climb up on the diving board before I went up the ladder the life guard asked me if I knew how to swim I told him yes. I knew it was a lie. I continued up the ladder and got to the top. I remember looking down into the water for a few moments. I knew then I wanted to die some kind of way and drowning was an easy way for me to do it. It doesn't take long for the water to fill up your lungs. I walk to the edge of the board closed my eyes and jumped in. I remember hitting the water and going down I just closed my eyes and fell my way to the bottom of the pool. I don't know how long it was but they seen me floating towards the bottom of the pool and one of the life guards jumped in to get me out the pool. The next thing I remember I was on the side of the pool getting my chest pumped in and kids standing around looking. His name was Earl he was the one who got me out the pool that day. He was one of our summer counselors. He was black like tar, very tall and cute for a super dark boy. I didn't know rather to be happy or sad that he saved my life that day. He wrapped me up in the towel and carried to a bench and told me to rest for a few moments. And then tells me to stay in front of him on the edge of the pool for the rest of the day.

After I released this part of my life to him I let out a long overdue sigh of relief. Still wrapped in his arms a dead silence comes into the room and I drift off to sleep.

A couple of days went by and neither one of us mentioned what was said a few nights ago. Being intimate is not an option. I guess he was able to see the pain in my eyes and knew that I still had more to tell. Night time comes again and I curl up in arms and ask him if he wanted to hear more. “Well if you feel like you have to talk about it then I will listen” he replied while adjusting himself as I curled up under him. “Here we go” I replied as I continued my story.

Part 2

Through the eyes of a jealous girl

Fear

Alone in a quiet room surrounded
By a sea of darkness and covered
By a mist of fear

I sit screaming in an empty
Chamber that no one else can hear

Scars so deep that they have cut
Through my very soul leaving me
With nothing but pain and fear

Defeat fills my body as my
Screams fills the room that
Only he can hear

I am bound down by a demon that
Only my eyes can see he likes
That and he can smell my fear

I'm tired as I watch the blood
Seep through my wounds as my
Soul slips away and my screams
I no longer hear

I have breast now like every girl in my neighborhood and I have hair down below. I have a big booty. I was pretty well that is what I was always told. But whenever I looked in the mirror I hated what I saw. My mom had candles and when we would go to the thrift store I would buy candles. I would tell her I wanted them so I could decorate my room. In private I would melt the wax and pour it on my breast and over my vagina. My uncle was hurting me and it was because I had breast and a vagina. So I was hurting them as a type of punishment for them. I would pour hot wax on my legs, arms, and even my face. The wax would just cool and fall off the pain only last a few moments. It wouldn't leave any permit scars but to me that was their punishment. That was the only punishment I could do to keep my secret from coming out. Inside my soul knew something was wrong but I had no way of getting it out. No way to explain it without someone being mad at me so I created a time bomb.

My mom sees some bloody underwear in the hamper I forgot to throw them out in the garage into the big trash can. She doesn't explain to me what it is called or what is the purpose or when does it come. Nothing. She doesn't even ask me how long has this been going on or did something cause it to happen. She takes a big box of pads and puts them on my bed and say “use them”. “When I was down south I had to use old dresses and rags for a pad”. I didn’t need to hear about what you used show me how to use the item properly that we have today. I was scared to tell her that it had been going on for a while and that my uncle caused it to happen. I didn’t want to get him in trouble or have him be mad at me for telling. So since my mother didn’t ask me any questions I didn’t have to tell her a lie.

And like a child who can’t hold water she runs and tell her sister. “She started her period”. She tells that bitch everything. Can we keep at least one secret dam between us. Everything I do she tells her. When I get in trouble she tells her. When I get good grades in school she tells her. When I have a fight with someone in the neighborhood she tells her. There is nothing she doesn’t tell her sister. And yes we can keep secrets I am at the time keeping a secret and my mother will continue to keep secrets.

My friend at school explain to me that I was on my period or menstruation now. My momma didn’t even tell me that. I wore some white jeans to school one day while on my period. And had an embarrassing moment well a trial and error moment. One of my girl friends at school saved me with a long sweater. She had me to tie it around my waist for the rest of the school day. She told me about every 3 hours change my pad and that my period comes every month on the same day until I get old and die. So I have to bleed for the next 100 years. My momma didn't even mention that to me but she was quick to tell her sister I started. But wasn't quick to tell me what to do and what not to do. Like don't wear white jeans would have been nice to know.

My friend told me I was now becoming a woman whatever that met. And to better protect myself if I could wear dark jeans or dresses during that time of the month just in case an accident happens again. As far as I know my mom must don't have a period because she hasn't said anything to me about it yet. She just tells me the pads are in the cabinet in the bathroom don't flush them down the toilet but wrap them up and put them in the trash can. She didn't even tell me what to do when I went to bed. And how to keep from messing up the sheets while I slept. Instead she got mad that I messed up her mattress she cussed me out while scrubbing out the blood stain. So again trial and error find an old towel fold it up and lay on it or get a plastic garbage bag and put that under your sheets. Who explained this to me my school friends. My mother just complained about how expensive buying them every month would be. And tell me stories of how they had to use old rags or old dresses and put them between their legs when they had their period because they were too poor to buy pads. "How would you like to have an old dress between your legs? And then having to re-fold it throughout the day. And then having to wash it out at night so you could wear it in the morning". I got so tired of her saying that to me. I swear sanitary napkins cost a million dollars the way she complained.

One of my uncle's girlfriends comes up with a baby and says it is his. She lives downstairs from my Great Aunt. I use to see her when I would go over to her house I didn't know that she knew my uncle. But come to find out they went to high school together. The baby is a boy he is very light skinned with bright red hair like an Irish man. And has a face full of freckles. My uncle doesn't say anything about it he is out of town somewhere he has joined the military. My mom went to get the baby one time for a day. She looked at him and spent the whole day on the phone telling relatives what the little baby looks like. Red hair runs on my uncle side of the family. I have a bunch of relatives with red hair and freckles. And after that day I never saw the little baby again. My mother never went back to get him I don't know why and never asked and never worried about it. And a matter of fact his mother has 3 kids and all their daddy's are 1st cousins I guess she wanted to keep it all in the family. Not only are they brother and sister but also first cousins. She also had children by my Great Aunt grandson.

I am learning about sex in health class in school and by gossiping with my friends. I'm in the 7th grade now. When a boy puts his dick in you its called sex, intercourse, love making or fucking. You can pick which word you what to chose. Girls in school that are doing this are talked about and called nasty, bitches, hoes or sluts depends on who is doing the talking. So I say "I haven't done it yet" whenever my friends ask me have I don't it yet. I don't want to get talked about in school or in the neighborhood so I keep what me and my uncle do to myself. I learned that when you have sex the girl gets pregnant almost every time. Now I am wondering why I haven't gotten pregnant by my uncle yet.

Well in this day and age its double dutch, hide and seek and drill team for fun neighborhood activities. These are the times were we had fun without the video games and internet. When we were able to play and run up and down the street without a drive by happening or a crack head trying to rob you. I am wearing French braids with beads and aluminum foil wrapped around the tips. My mom lets a girl on our street braid my hair for the summer that way she doesn't have to do my hair every day. But who ever thought of putting a small piece of aluminum foil at the end of a braid instead of rubber bands was stupid. But we all did it if you were black so what is that telling you? It was a black thing.

My father finally agreed to let me have a bang. He almost had a cow when my mother cut my hair in the front to make the small bangs in front of my head. The hair came to end of my nose and to him that was still too short. But when I got my bangs I thought I was the shit even thou I needed bobby pins to hold it up and keep it out my face. My dad didn't want it cut any shorter. It was either the length he agreed to or not at all.

I see my half sister less and less she is about three years older than me. We are both in high school but we go to different ones. Some of the people at my high school know her because they live in the same neighborhood as she does. But she never mentions me as being her younger half sister so the people in my high school think I am lying. I guess jealously can make some people act ugly. She definitely inherited the ugly acting part from our dad side of the family.

But I remember this one time I had went to a high school track meet. I went by myself but I knew my half sister and her cousins would be there. Well it was some girls from my high school there that did not like me why just because. I didn't know these girls from Adam. One didn't like me because they claim I stole another girl's hair style. I seen her rocking this hair style and I decided to wear my hair the same way who in the hell has copy rights over a hair style maybe I looked better than she did with it. Then I had her little entrouge not liking me it was like this from the first day I attended that high school. I got the dirty looks and the smart comments when I walked by. Then I heard the rumors that I was stuck up and conceited. Which was not the case I just don't mingle with people I am not comfortable with I stay away and keep to myself until I find someone I am comfortable with talking to. I didn't come there with an entrouge my eighth grade class all got split up throughout the city attending different high school. I was the only girl from my middle school to be attending this high school. So I was basically a loner. But these immature people saw it as me being stuck up and conceited because I didn't run around mingling with everyone. So after this particular track meet the entrouge of girl who were also the track runners and some were on the school drill team sent me a message that the little leader was going to kick my ass after the track meet. The girl was little, short and skinny had a lot of mouth and was popular. If she didn't like you then none of her faithful followers would either. So I walked over to my half sister and I told her what was said to me. She said "okay this is what I want you to do. When the track meet is over I want you to walk out of the stadium like you always do and don't worry'. This was the first time I had ever run to my half sister for help. I did as she told me to. The leader of group along with her entrouge decided to form a circle around me in the middle of the street while I walked to the bus stop. They was talking shit to me calling me bitches talking about they were going to fuck me up. I was one person surrounded by 10 girls who all agreed to not like me because their leader didn't isn't this the same stupid shit the German Nazi's did with Hitler? But not one of them step to the middle of the circle to fight me not one of them took the first step to beat my ass but they all hated me. Not even the loud mouth leader who talked more shit than a little bit about me but the only thing she knew about me was my name. But she hated me like I stole something from her ass. So my sister, her cousins and her friends from her high school came out the stadium and formed a circle around them. My sister told them "if any of you got beef with my sister you got beef with us". No one said a word they mumble a few things and broke their circle and walked off. Things changed a little bit in high school between me and my entrouge of haters. They still gave me the dirty looks and eye rolling but they did not say one word to me.

Then about 12 years later I went to go sign up for some health insurance for my children. Since I was considered to have a low income home I qualified for some free health insurance for my children I would still have to pay for own coverage but for my children it was free. I received the letter in the mail tell me to bring in certain documentation and my case worker name was no other than the loud mouth leader from high school. I laughed because "I was like this can't be the same chick that couldn't stand me in high school". So I went to the interview I signed in and showed the front desk lady my letter and who I was there to see. Now when you are guilty of some foul bullshit you never know how to face the other person. I saw her when she came out to look to see if I was there. I was the only person in the room. It was her alright she a very distinctive birth mark on her face. I guess when she put my name and face together she realized who I was. She went to the back and gave my case to another person. Why she couldn't face me I don't know I never had a problem with her personally but that little entrouge she was in had a problem with me. So when I was called to the back to see my new case worker I made it a point to go and stand in front of her office door and when she looked up I smiled and walked away. Sometimes no words are the best words.

My dad is still drinking but he has stop running us out of the house since we moved. He was forty-five when I was born. And even in his old age he looked fine. So I could just imagine how he must have looked in his glory years. I saw a picture of him when he was younger in his army clothing. He was average looking slender and he had that light skin and silky black hair. He was a cutie pie but he was also abusive. My mother wore a partial. She told me my father had gotten mad at her when they first met and punched her in the mouth and knocked out her tooth. She told me how the people at her job were laughing at her because they knew he did it. When I was born I think his fire was physical abuse was just about out. So when a person loses strength in one area they regain it in another area. And his new area of attack on her was verbal abuse. I have plenty of memories were he would just look at her and start calling her ugly. We would be watching a nature program on television and if a monkey was on program he would say "doesn't that look just like your momma. Look at her that monkey looks just like her". He would then laugh and then I would laugh. If she was hurt about his comments she hailed it in. Sometimes I would catch her crying about the things he has said about her. "Why is he doing this to me? He is too old for this shit" she would say. I had no answer for her I just couldn't understand why she had allowed it for so many years. Forty years of abuse she took from him. The physical, mental and emotional torture he place upon her. When he did start giving her compliments it was because of old age. His fire was all out and he had no choice but to say nice things to her. Or maybe guilty has set in. Her is a woman I tortured for forty years now that I am close to death let me start being nice to her. But he was also very careful to never abuse her in front of her family. In their eyes he was the greatest man on the planet. He worked a nice job and he had brought a nice home. My mother was always sending boxes of clothing to them every other week. When someone in the family needed money he was always there. He was great he was a charmer. But they didn't know was the things that went on behind the doors back at home.

But now when he throws a fit but my mom just goes upstairs or goes outside in the backyard until he cools off. But I remember one morning I was around 12 I think and I heard some noise coming from my parent's room. I remember my dad had been drinking the night before. When I went to bed around midnight he was still downstairs drinking. My mother had already left and went to bed hours before me because she could not take my father's cussing anymore. So I went to my parents bedroom and opened the door and seen my dad but ass naked tied to the bed. I can't remember exactly what was around his arms and legs but he looked like Jesus on the cross. My mother was also but ass naked. She was on top of him beating the shit out of him. I closed the door and went back to my room and jumped back into the bed and pulled the covers over my head. Later on that day my dad looked like a truck ran him over and went 3 times in reverse to make sure his as was run over. He had scratches and marks all over his yellow ass. I remember he told his brother that he got drunk and fell down the stairs but I knew and my mother knew what happened. While he was telling the story he was looking at me to make sure I didn't but into the conversation and corrected him. Then my uncle would know the truth. He got his ass whooped and was too drunk to put the pieces together and when he did put them together it was too late she had him tied up like a wild hog. For the next couple of days he would bring my mother homes red roses and she would just throw them on the floor. I went to pick them up and she told me to leave them there. This went on for a couple of days. I don't know what that met but he kept buying roses and she keep throwing them on the floor. Well the good thing was he stop acting like a fool with his drinking he said the doctor told him to cut back or maybe it was the ass kicking he got. I never figured out what exactly happened but I guess my mom had an Ike and Tina moment and beat that ass 20 years in the making. But my dad is about 20 years older than my mom. And at this time she is still working 2nd shift to avoid his bullshit which is cool because he learned to finally have 1 drink and shut up and sit it down. But he is now on her mercy because he has no job.

My uncle has another girlfriend she doesn't live in the same city as we do. She lives in Niagara Falls and sometimes he catches the greyhound to her house. They go to college together. She is nice but dam she got some thick ass glasses, short hair and beaver teeth. She plays basketball just like he does.

Personally he could have done better if you go by looks. But she was always nice to me and my parents. But my jealously took over and I chose not to like her because she was my uncle's girlfriend. Now why would he want to fuck her? She is so ugly and I am way prettier I would think to myself. When she leaves I walk around the house imitating her to my parents because she talks funny with her beaver teeth. Me and my mother sit in the kitchen and make fun of the way she looks and talks. My mother always says "I don't know why he is with her she is ugly". But back then I thought that you should be with someone based on looks. She was a very nice person and I know she caught me making fun of her a few times but still treated me nice. We never said anything other than hi and bye to one another but she was always polite.

But little did I know that I was starting to act like a jealous girlfriend. In my mind I hated what he did to me but I didn't want him doing it to anyone else either. My mind hadn't quiet realized what had been happening to me. Yes he was my uncle but in a sick way I started claiming him as my man in my head because of what we did together. I could not at this point in my life comprehend in my mind that what he did to me was wrong because in a sick way to me we did things that lovers did or husband and wives or girlfriend and boyfriends. On television you always saw people who were in love doing what we did together. In my mind I felt that he did those things to me because he loved me. Not because he was a sick pervert. No one never taught me or told me what a pervert was. And at this time it wasn't on television. I heard of rape being on the news but no one ever taught me what rape was either.

My eyes could not see the monster in front of me taking advantage of me every chance he got. When you don't talk to someone about what is going on in your life things like this happen. My mother never talked to me about boys and what boys and girls did together. Or what it was you were and were not suppose to do with a boy. I started to form a curtain around what was really happening to me. My mother was going through her own thing with my dad and other family member's issues. Every week it was always something that was pissing her off or making her upset. She wanted as less drama as possible even if that meant not talking to me about life. All she did was bury herself in her books. She had stacks of books on her table. When she wasn't being a slave for my father or working she was somewhere buried in a book reading.

So I started developing my jealous streak. My dad didn't pay it any attention he was sleep from drinking or was gone fishing or just thought I was being a pain in the ass towards my uncle. My mom well I only saw her on the weekends so she didn't notice my jealous streak just thought I was being funny or acting spoiled. Everyone around me thought just because I was the only child that I was a spoiled brat. And that I had this attitude about me because I was a spoil person. They never thought anything was wrong. Look she has everything a child her age could want.

I would tear up things in his room whenever I was home alone. I would go through his things in his dresser mess up his papers for school. Cut up his college books or rip out pages in the book. I would even take all the shoes laces out of his sneakers and throw them away. I would do anything to be a little bitch towards him. He didn't say one word to my parents about the shit I was doing. I guess he didn't want his cover blown. I guess he knew I was a ticking time bomb and he knew sooner or later I was going to explode. It was time to wean me.

He would give me dirty looks but he knew not to say anything. He had a job at a pizza shop and would buy things to try and calm me down but that only worked for a moment. The gifts didn't stop me it just gave me a reason to cuss him out when he didn't have anything to give me. When he didn't have money to give me. That is when I asked for it I behaved like a woman in rage. No one thought it was strange again they all thought I was just being a spoiled brat.

At this time I was becoming a woman almost 13. I had a small body but a mouth like an old drunk woman when I felt like releasing it. I knew how to cuss been cussing since I could remember and whenever we were alone I made sure I cussed him out like he belonged to me. He didn't say anything back to me he knew better. I guess he thought I would slip up one day and say he is fucking me to too his girlfriend so he chose not to argue back with me.

I guess the college life isn't going as he planned. So he drops out of college and signs up for the military to be in the Air Force. And his girlfriend well she did also maybe because he did it. I could tell by their love letters that they were planning a life together. Both have military careers. She was very smart so I don't know why she would drop out of college to follow him. She has no idea what she is following. Yes he is good looking but she doesn't know what he is.

He doesn't fuck me as much as he did before but it's okay. He joins the military and I don't see him for a while. He is in boot camp I think for a few weeks away somewhere I don't know. But he calls my mom and dad on a regular. So my mind begins to bury all that has been happening to me. Maybe because he's is not there to remind me of the memories that I already have. Or maybe by me going to church every Sunday is helping me through this somehow. Maybe by me going to church God had a chance to renew my spirit and increase my strength for the week. Or God could have been blinding me to the situation I was in.

Right now it's is an out of sight and out of mind situation. So who cares who he is fucking in the military it doesn't matter because he isn't around me. My mind is now preoccupied with another person.

A new guy moved into our neighborhood he is from another country so he talks with an accent. He looks okay but I think it's his voice that attracts me to him more than anything else. A lot of people are impressed by the clothes we wears and the jewelry he has. He does the things boys do when they like you. Like walk past your house a thousand times when you're sitting on the porch and looks at you. How cute and innocent that use to be. When your friends would tease you about some guy liking you and we would sit together and giggle about it.

I would watch him play football with the other boys and try to be a show off and fuck up the play every time or drop the ball. I would walk down to the field down the street and watch him play. I would be his personal cheer leader. Then one day we exchanged phone numbers after weeks of sneaking in little conversations outside here and there. We talked on the phone but if I was on the phone more than 15 minutes my dad would be screaming for me to get off the phone. And god forbid if the phone rang again after I just hung it up his ass would have a fit. We didn't have a 2-way line like some of my friends so talking on the phone for a long time I couldn't do it. And a cell phone or a personal computer to email someone that wasn't even thought of back then.

Around this time my parents are taking care of foster kids. My dad company was sold and he lost his job after being there for over 20 years. They needed to supplement the lost income. My mom still worked second shift so all she had to do was put them on the bus in the morning. She cooked dinner so when I got home from school all I had to do was warm up dinner in the microwave and gets them off the school bus and then make sure their homework was done then give them a bath and do their hair and put them to bed. Doing any after school activities or joining any clubs at my high school was a negative because I had to take care of the kids. Whenever I asked about joining a club or an afterschool activity the first thing to come out of my parents mouths was "I need you to come straight home to watch these kids". My dad wasn't going to do it but he agreed to take care of them. He was drinking, sleep or gone fishing or watching television. And if I even thought about going somewhere on the weekend my ass had to take them with me how convenient. Why because my dad wasn't going to watch and my mother was at work but they signed up to care for them.

Even on the weekends if I went somewhere to hang out with my friends they were tagging along like to little orphans. If I went to go met my boyfriend I had to buy them candy to be quiet about it. The first thing they would say "I am telling". I meet a lot of different kids through this foster care program who had some fucked up family problems or had mental problems of their own. I did form relationships with some of them even after they moved on and went back to their biological family we still keep in touch and laugh about some of the things they did as children. On the holidays sometimes they would call or come by the house to visit. They called me their sister when they stayed with us and even after they weren't in my parents care anymore we still consider ourselves to be sisters.

So now I have me a boyfriend and since I am a part time nanny we meet up when we can he is 3 years older than me. I see him in the morning before I go to school he has a car so he drives me and picks me up from school sometimes depending on how his college class schedule is like. He has a stick shift in his car and my favorite car a Mustang. He taught me how to drive it so sometimes he lets me drives while he be the passenger. Everything is innocent we kiss all the time and write letters to one another. Like every other male on this dam planet he comes with the same dam question "when are we going to have sex". I can't be mad it did take him almost a year to finally ask me. But me being alone with him was almost impossible.

My mom brought me a diary one day out of the blue. It was white trimmed in gold. It had a lock on front of it. You couldn't open it unless you had a key or if you took the time to rip off the front cover. So every time I seen my little boyfriend I would write about it in my diary. It's private its mine so nobody need to be reading my shit right?

Now that I think about it that was her way of seeing what was going on in my life instead of talking to me or teaching me about life. She brought my adopted sister a diary also when she was around 13. And one day when she was gone somewhere she ripped off the cover and read her diary. Then when she read it she was upset. I remember she called me and told me "she is having sex and sneaking around to be with a boy and lying to me about being in all these school activities". I asked her how did she know and she told me "ripped open her diary and read it". She called her every bitch in the world just like she did me. I had already talked to my sister about sex and I told my mother she needed to get her on birth control her response was "she isn't thinking about sex". Boy was she wrong but that's another story.

Meanwhile my uncle is busy with his new military career. He comes home every now and then for visits. And he stays a few days and go back to his station. Since my parents have foster kids now trying to fuck me well that has become a hard task for him to figure out. It didn't stop him it just made him slicker at it. I had the body of a woman now. If he was attracted to me before puberty what makes you think he isn't now?

Now my little boyfriend and I are getting along just fine no arguments no disagreements. We sit and talk about future bullshit and the fairy tale life of living happily ever after. We talk about where we want to live, the type of car we want to have and how many kids. We even talk about our wedding the colors who will be in it. We even go as far as to plan our honeymoon all sorts of bullshit fantasies that will never happen. But at this moment in time its fun pretending.

We talk about sex and make plans to finally have sex with one another. He asks me "are you a virgin" I replied to him "yes". I know at this time in my life what a virgin was and what it meant to be one. I knew that my uncle was fucking me which made me not be a virgin. But in my mind a part of me kept acting like none of that counted like none of it happened. Like I was still pure and untouched. Maybe I started blocking it out to protect me and not him. Or maybe my mind or even God knew that I couldn't handle the truth right now. Maybe I developed some kind of split personality at this point in my life. You had this one girl who was innocent in her family eyes, her boyfriend eyes, and her friends even to the foster children who counted on me more than I knew. Then you had this other girl who was a straight up slut for her uncle who made her that way. So the innocent girl put on a "persona" that she is "untouched" to protect the slut who was violated, embarrassed, confused and hurt and couldn't handle the truth right now.

It's Halloween and there is a party happening at the recreation center in our neighborhood which is about a 10 minute walk from my house. My parents never let me go anywhere without the little orphans. So I have one of my girlfriends that lived on my street to help beg my parents into letting me go without the orphans. Well we tell my mom that her older brother is going to walk us to and from the party and we will be back around 9:00 p.m.

Since her brother his friends with my boyfriends he agrees to tell the lie to my mother. We tell her it's for teenager's and that the little orphans can't go but I will take them trick-or-treating before I leave. My mom finally agrees to let me go but I had plans of being alone with my boyfriend. His mother and sister were out of town this weekend it's just him and his older brother there at the house. It's around 7:00 p.m. we leave and I go to his house and my girlfriend goes to someone else's house. We promise to meet up at 8:30 p.m so we can walk home together.

So we are alone for the first time and he tried to do the romantic things he had on music, candles and Halloween candy for me. He has already given me the "it might hurt" speech at least 100 times and I get it another "it might hurt" speech 100 more times tonight. I wore a pair of blue jeans and a yellow shirt with flower prints on it. I didn't wear any sexy underwear I don't think I owned any Victoria secret at that age. We kiss as usual he touched me everywhere which was a first because we had never been alone before to do this. This was the first time we had ever seen each other naked.

He looked at me by candle light. To me that was so romantic. He kissed and sucked on my breast. That was the first time anybody has ever done that. My uncle fucked me but he never kissed my lips or my breast. It was more like get over here his pants are down and I get fucked and he sends me about my way. Or he would just shove his dick down my throat until he got his enjoyment.

No romance there. But this was romantic. I knew it was wrong because I was being sneaky and creeped over to his house. But I had no freedom and every time I looked around I was being a nanny to the foster kids. Now to me he cared about me because he tried to make it as special as possible for me. My uncle never did anything like that for me. He didn't care if I was comfortable or not.

So now he is naked lying next to me. He puts on his condom we had the condom talk 100 times before now I have to get it 100 times tonight. I wonder in my head while all of this is going on why my uncle never used a condom with me. Did he use condoms with his other girlfriends? My boyfriend knew about condoms because he had a child at a very young age and didn't want that mistake to happen again. We proceed to have sex. He gets on top of me and gives me the "it's going to hurt speech" 100 times and then he finally put his dick inside of me. I don't even think I made a sound or moved. He did ask me again was I "a virgin" and I reassured him that I was. He asked me that a couple of times that night and I started to get mad and agitated with him. I told him "why would I lie about it" And he was like "I'm just wondering that's all". We finished and then he ran and got his version of a romantic dinner microwave pizza and soda under candlelight. It was cute 20 years ago if a man did that today I would probably knock his dam head off. He made the evening special and in my book he got an A+ for that. Even thou I had already been violated by my uncle to me this was the first time.

We did continue to date for a while after that over a year. The sex didn't change anything between us and he didn't go running his mouth about what happened between us either. My parent s weren't about to let me date or go out with him somewhere. My parents did not like him at all and I never knew why. So we would met when we could at the mall on Saturday, high school football games, or at high school track meets when ever my parents would let me go to one. This went on for about one year.

I continued to see my boyfriend and now it's almost close to our first year together. And one morning in the middle of breakfast I began throwing up all over the kitchen floor. I have never been sick before. I normally don't get sick. My parents said it must have been something I ate and everyone brushed it off and I go and lay down for the rest of the day.

A friend of mine from school was having a sweet 16 birthday party. My parents never let me go anywhere because they want to be stuck watching those foster kids they signed up for. But my parents agreed to let me go to the sleepover but said they will be back early in the morning to get me they didn't drop me off until 9 P.M when the foster kids went to bed. I'm excited because I have never spent the night at anyone house before. Every time I ask the answer was always no so this time its yes I could almost die!

Well I guess my mom finally realized that she hasn't brought me any maxi pads in a while. I think that is what triggered her off. Or maybe I was away from the house and that gave her a chance to read my diary to see what I have been up to. But I never even thought about my period being missed or not coming hell I was sick of it anyway. And my mother never said what it met when you missed your period hell she never talked to me about what the function of it was. So while I am at the sleep over I guess my mother who has never talked to me about boys, sex, or even my dam menstruation decides to take her black rusty ass up in my room and rip off the cover of my diary. She read about how I sneak to see my boyfriend before I go to school and what we do together and all of that stuff.

So it's about 8 in the morning and my dad is at the door to come get me. Its super early I think we had just gone to sleep. All of my friends were still laying around the house sleep. I feel something is wrong as soon as I looked at the truck. My mom is in the truck and she won't even speak to me or look at me. My dad well he was till acting the same. We drive home the whole trip is in silence. No one asks about the party did I like it did I not. I am sitting in the back seat wondering what those little orphans told to get me in trouble. We get home I walk into the house and the first thing I see on the kitchen table is my diary.

The cover was ripped off my diary. My father goes and sits down in his chair in front of the television. And my mother yells at me "you're pregnant" and "that's why I haven't brought any dam maxi pads for your nasty ass". Then she said "I read your little book you nasty bitch".

The little foster girls are home they are about 10 years younger than me. They are upstairs in their room and I am sure they heard everything that was said and probably don't understand what it is that they are hearing. I don't know if they understood it or not I never asked them about what they heard. My mother called me everything but a child of God that day. I was a hoe, slut, bitch, and a tramp, stupid, nasty and I wasn't going to be shit. My mother has never called me out of my name in my 15 years of living. But today was the day I lost my mother. Not physically but mentally and emotionally I don't know which one is worse. To have someone in your life physically that is dead or in the ground dead. She hated me from that day forth. And I don't know if she was madder at herself than at me. My dad didn't say a word he just had a sad look on his face. I never got a chance to open my mouth to defend myself. She never asked me about what was in that book she never asked me why I was sneaking around. She shouted she screamed she threw things around the house. My dad just sat in his chair until finally he told her that was enough and sent me upstairs to my room. I went upstairs in my room and as I was about to go into my room I seen the little orphans standing in the doorway with tears in their eyes. I went in my room and laid across my bed. I could still here my parents downstairs arguing but I could not make out exactly what was being said.

My mom came upstairs a few moments later. I hear her go into the bathroom and turn on the water in the bath tub. The two little girls are still in their room. I think my mother told them not to come out for a while. I heard her close the door to their room. She turns the water on in the tub and it's super hot. She calls me into the bathroom and asks me to take my clothes off in front of her and I did. Then she pushes me into the tub with the hot water. I remember screaming because the water was so dam hot. I remember her pushing me back into the water when I tried to get out of the tub. She was telling me to "wash you nasty ass you bitch" and I was just a "filthy hoe" I don't know how long it went on. But finally my dad came into the bathroom and told her that was enough. My mom told me "don't you ever put your nasty hands on me again". And I have never touched my mother nor has she touched me in any form in over 23 years. That was her wish not mine. No more hugs or kisses and no more "I love you". It was a done deal between me and her. I tired later on in the years to get a touch from her but whenever I tried to hug her she would push me away. To her I am filth and my presence in her life is tolerated because unfortunately I just happen to be her daughter. I hear her tell other people all the time on the phone or in person that she "loves" them. I can look her straight in the eyes today and tell her "I love you" and get no response from her just a blank stare back. The child in me just holds on to the memories when we use to hug and kiss. The fun times when we use to dance together. And sing together our made up songs and silly dances. The child in me in some messed up way is still begging for her forgiveness 23 years later. Just so she would hug me again or even say she loves me again. I cry a lot for her to be my old mother again to accept me again, but one day she may cry for me but will I be there will I even hear her? She may even need me to hold her one last time but will I be there?

I am finally sent to my room after the chaos in the bathroom. I am devastated beyond belief mentally. But I refuse to let my mother see me cry. I refuse to breakdown in front of her some call it pride and some call it strength. But I knew right then that I will not give this bitch the satisfaction of seeing me cry after what she did to me. She always said tears were a sign of weakness and even at my lowest point I refuse to cry especially in front of her and because of her.

My dad tells me he is going to my boyfriend house to talk to him and his mother about this pregnancy. Neither my mother or my dad never asked me who was it that I was having sex with. That is why you are not supposed to assume nothing. I don't know what was said between my father and my boyfriend and his mother. Neither him nor my boyfriend ever discusses with me what was exchanged between them. But I know the baby I was carrying was not his. He always used a condom and my uncle never did when he had sex with me. I may have written down in my diary what

I did with my boyfriend I just didn't add the fact that we used condoms. Again they just assumed we had unprotected sex.

Now I am called downstairs to get another round of torture from my mother. She cusses me out about being pregnant then I get cussed out again because she has to pay for me to have an abortion. And how much this abortion is going to cost her. Not once did this selfish bitch ever ask me how I felt. No one ever asked if I wanted to keep the baby or who was the father. So after standing in the middle of the floor for about 2 hours maybe more and being belittled I was sent upstairs for the next 2 days. I just left my room to use the bathroom and nothing else. My father would bring food upstairs in the middle of the night. He was always the last one to come upstairs and go to bed.

Abortion. I heard of it but I never really knew exactly what it meant or what it was. I never had any friends bring up that word in conversation so I am lost as to what exactly this is. I have no one to ask what does this mean I have to have an abortion. My mother won't talk to me about it and my dad hasn't said a word to me either about this abortion. So this will be another trial and error.

My mom tells me to get up and get ready so she can take me to the abortion clinic. This is the first time she has spoken to me in 2 days. We go to the abortion clinic there were protesters outside. They were holding up signs and screaming at the girls that entered the door "Don't kill your baby". I am saying what the hell in my head. My dad goes next door to a café'. My mom walks me into the abortion clinic gives the lady at the front window her credit card and tells me to stay here until they call me and then she leaves. There are a lot of girls and grown women here at the clinic. They are black, white, all races of women in the waiting room. Some were alone and some were not. Some you were able to tell were pregnant and some you cannot. The room is silent everyone in there has a sad or distraught look on their face. No one is even talking to one another mainly we are all looking at the clock on the wall or looking at the ground. I am finally called to the back after sitting there for about an hour. I don't know rather to be happy or sad. They tell me I have to take a urine test to tell if I am pregnant or not. After my urine test came back positive I then go to another room where I had to talk to a counselor. She asked me over and over was I being forced to have a procedure done. I reassured her that I was not but I don't think she was happy with my body language. She started talking to me about adoption options and welfare assistance. But my mother had already told me not to leave the building without getting it done. At this moment in time I feared my mother more than anything. After talking to her for about twenty minutes I went to another room to get a sonogram done. The lady in the sonogram room was nice to me. I asked if I could see the image of my baby. It was the first time I had seen a picture of a baby on a sonogram machine. I have 4 children now of my own and I have seen plenty of sonograms but this one sonogram encounter will always stay in my mind. My first child I thought to myself. The lady tells me it is a girl. My daughter I think and in my mind I name her. Her father is a monster and it's not her fault that she was conceived.

The lady tells me I am about 14 weeks pregnant. And I would have to have a two day procedure instead of a one day procedure. I still do not fully understand what is about to happen to me or my baby. All I can do is shake my head into agreement with everything she says to me. Even though I do understand I still shake my head in agreement. I go into another room and I lay on the table and she explains to me that a device is going to be inserted inside of me to help dilate and I will be back in the morning to get the procedure finished. In my mind I still don't know what is really going on. A few hours have gone by maybe about 6 hours. I leave the abortion clinic and my parents are waiting for me in the truck. My dad is silent but my mother cussed and complained the whole way home. "Now I have to pay extra because you need a two day procedure" and "if we would have waited any longer you would have had to have that damn baby" and "who is going to replace this money I am spending on this". Not once did this selfish inconsiderate bitch ask me "how you feel" are you okay are you scared. Instead of one of them being with me to help explain what was about to happen they chose to sit in the café and sip on coffee. Not one word of sympathy came from my mother's mouth. She didn't even have the compassion to sit with me in the waiting room. There were women in the waiting room who were with their mothers or a sister or even a close friend. Some had either their boyfriend or husbands with them. I was the only one in that room alone.

I lay in my bed that night alone, scared and confused. My baby kicked the whole night this was the first time I actually felt her there. I don't think I slept at all that night. I laid there in my bed holding on to my stomach while the baby kicked. I didn't know she was kicking because she was inside of me fighting for her life. I could hear my mother bitching the whole night. I was begging God to not let me wake up because I didn't want to see my mother again. I kept telling my baby I was so sorry please forgive me. A part of me wanted to run away but I had no place to run to.

My security blanket was gone. Cleo had been dead for 2 years now. She was about 14 years old and had developed some cancerous tumors in her stomach. You could see the knots in her abdomen. I would rub her stomach and I would feel them. Instead of putting the dog out of her misery and letting the veterinarian put her down they let her live and suffer until she died. I remember my mother complaining about how much it would cost and that dogs were too expensive to have. I don't know how much it cost to put a dog down but she did not deserve the misery she suffered at the end of her life. And I remember my parents and my uncle having to carry her outside to use the bathroom because she could no longer go down and up the stairs. Even to the end she would still try and crawl to me when she saw me still trying to comfort me and protect me even when she couldn't walk anymore. When she died I knew what it finally felt like to lose something precious. She wasn't human at all but she was my protector she knew what I was going through when I was home alone with my uncle. She couldn't talk to me but I could talk to her and having her lay up under me at night knowing she was there to protect me gave me all the comfort in the world. When I would cry she would lick my tears away I didn't even mind dog slob all over my face. To her I was her baby she had been trained from birth to protect me and she did a good job giving me comfort. Even thou I had no words to explain how I felt and what I was going through my dog Cleo knew how to comfort me. And now I didn't have her. I didn't have anyone or anything to comfort me at this moment in time.

The next day the same treatment no words spoken between me and my parents. We go to the abortion clinic and they go to the café next door. I walk into the abortion clinic alone. The protestors are outside again today and I am given a pamphlet by one of them. It had images of aborted fetuses on it and that is when reality hit me. This is what I was about to do to my daughter. I haven't felt her move since late last night. A part of me prayed that she was already dead inside of me and wouldn't be able to feel this fate I had put upon her. Even though it was not my choice. I must have told God a million times over I was sorry but I have no choice and just please forgive me.

I was called to the back after about an hour of waiting. I laid on the table and put my feet in the stir ups as instructed. I see the lady from yesterday she explains to me the procedure and how it will only be a few seconds and that I wouldn't feel anything. The doctor name was Payne he has his tag on his white jacket when he entered the room. He is an African American and rude as hell. The lady was trying to explain to me what was going to happen to me today. He interrupted her by saying "I don't have all day she should have kept her legs shut". She held my hand and told me to just keep looking at her. We stared at each other and when the sound of the vacuum came on I just started crying. It was something I had no choice in doing but was forced to do and regret it still dearly today. She wiped my tears and walked me to the back room of the clinic. The room was filled with women and girls of all nationalities lying on cots. We all had the look of guilt on our faces. Even thou everyone's reason was different for being at the clinic we all felt some sort of remorse. No one made eye contact with one another we were each ashamed of the choice we had made that day. The nurse walked me over to my cot. I laid down and she covered me with a small blanket and slept I for a few hours.

I woke up after a few hours of sleep and was told it was time for me to leave because I wasn't bleeding heavy and they would see me back in a week for a follow up appointment. The lady at the front desk gave me some papers and told me if I start to bleed heavy to go to the nearest emergency room. She handed me a card with my appointment on it and I left the clinic and walked to the truck my dad was there but my mom well I guess she decided to go to work instead of waiting on me. She didn't care if I lived or died from that day on. My feelings and well being at this point in time meant nothing to her.

Me and my dad go home he didn't say anything to me on the way home. I just sat in the back seat with an orange sleeping bag wrapped around me. I stared out the window trying to erase all that had just happened to me in the clinic. Trying to get the sonogram picture out of my head and trying to erase the sound of her heart beat that played in my mind. We get home and the two little crumb snatchers were there on the porch. My uncle that smells like pee-pee had watched them until we got back. I haven't seen or talked to them in a few days. They asked me how I was doing and I told them I was fine and I listened to them tell me about school and cartoons and the kids in their class and the ones on the bus that they don't like. How bad the kids on the bus were and how good they were. I listened as best as I could for a few minutes then went upstairs and went to my bedroom to lay down.

That night my dad came into my bedroom. He asked me if I was alright and told me that it would be okay. And that I was too young to be a mother. I was still in high school and didn't understand what it was like to raise a child. He told me that I had plenty of time to become a mother. That was fine he at least tried to ease the pain but he didn't know who the father of the baby was. I knew and my boyfriend knew that was not his baby the timing was off and when we had sex he used a condom every time. My dad reassured me that he loved me still and not to have sex with every guy I call my boyfriend. This was a nice conversation to have seeing that no one had spoken to me in about 5 days it was just good to know that my dad was not mad at me to the extent that my mother was and that in his heart and soul I was still his little girl even thou I did screw up and have sex with someone, that I lied and was sneaking to see him. At least it wasn't forced. Whatever I and my boyfriend did was because I wanted to.

The time has come I finally see my boyfriend after 2 weeks of not having any contact with him. The first thing he says is that he was sorry that I had to go through all of that by myself. We hugged for a few moments no words spoken. He just held me for a while I think I cried in his arms the whole time we were standing there. Then he finally says 'I am so sorry the condom broke I didn't know that it did" and I just said "It's okay". I never told him about my uncle so to him it was his fault. He had been completely faithful to me the whole time. If I am being force to have sex with my uncle then I am cheating on him? We continued our relationship there was no reason to sneak around and go to his house. My parents knew I was seeing him now but they still wouldn't let me go on a date with him or let him come to the house to see me. How stupid is that you already know we had sex you already know

I have been going to his house. But my mother did not want him nowhere near her home. If she came outside and seen him talking to me she would tell him to leave. So he mainly came around when my dad was home or when I was there by myself. My father didn't seem to be as angry towards him like my mother was. I wonder will she be this angry when she finds out about my uncle. But we stuck with one another for another year after that it wasn't the same though. I didn't want to be intimate with him anymore. I just slowly withdrew myself from him physically, mentally and emotionally.

My mother barely spoke to me after I had the abortion unless she really had to. And even then the conversation was short. Whenever she could she would pass by me like she didn't know me while we were in the same house. My dad would not show me any affection in front of her. If he hugged me or kissed me she would get a look of disgust all over her face. If me and him were joking and laughing about something she would get an instant attitude. So I slowly just stayed away from him in her presence. I didn't want him to get into it with her because he was still treating me like a daughter and not filth.

She usually tells her sister everything. But this abortion she kept in the household. It was between me, her and my father. Every chance she got she would bring it up. She charged it on her credit card and whenever she had to pay the bill that was her chance to bring it back up. "I still have this abortion bill to pay for. That was money I could have used on something else. But you wanted to go fuck around. That damn nigga you were sneaking around with his momma not helping me pay for this shit". She kept that memory alive forever. I couldn't heal when I am constantly being reminded about it all the time. Whenever she felt like throwing cheap shots at me she would. But she didn't run and gossip on the phone and tell her sister this time.

Well my mother gets a call from my uncle one day out of the blue. He tells her he is married now and he and his wife and step daughter are coming to visit for a few days. No one knew about this marriage I think they went downtown in there city or something and did it. They are both in the Air Force that is how they met. Now my mother is gossiping on the phone with her damn sister complaining about "who is this lady" and "how can he just up and marry someone that no one in the family has met or even heard of". "It's some woman he meets while being the military and she already has a baby by someone". "I didn't even know he broke up with his girlfriend they joined together". The gossip went on and on. Well I should be the first to welcome her to our happy family. What does she has that made him run off and marry her without telling anyone.

They came and the visit it was an okay meeting I guess. My mother asked her questions about her family and my dad was joking with my uncle and his new wife. And I was given the chore of keeping her daughter occupied. I keep my distance I didn't want to be around anyone so

I either stayed in my room or went outside in the backyard or on the porch. She has a 2 year old little girl she looks just like her mother. But in my mind I feel sorry for her I can just imagine what he is doing to her. When people have habits of doing things they aren't supposed to do they usually keep up the habit. They know it's wrong but in a sick kind of way they keep doing it either until they get caught or die whichever one comes first. So if he did it to me my guess is he is doing something to her also.

They leave after a few days. And my mother is back on the phone gossiping with her sister about the visit. "I don't like her" and "she is lazy she calls on him to do everything. She can't even cook". "She just wanted someone to marry her so they can take care of that little girl. And he was stupid enough to do it". My mother went on for hours complaining about her. But the whole time she was there my mother played in her face that she loved her. Well I can't worry about her or complain at least my mother mouth is occupied with a new victim.

It's my junior year of high school. I still have my neighborhood boyfriend but I don't want to be bothered with him. My mom says "he fucked you now got you pregnant and now he doesn't want you". But that wasn't the case at all. He didn't do one thing wrong to me but since I had that abortion I have never been the same when it came to us. I don't know what happened to me but I know I changed in some sort of way. So I finally decide to cut it off between us. I remember the day I did it.

We were at the corner of Elmwood and West Utica I was waiting on the bus to go home and he had met me there in his car. He was crying and asking me not to do this to him. He didn't do anything wrong he was apologizing for something he didn't even do. He kept asking me how could he fix it and the only thing I could tell him was that I didn't want to see him anymore I couldn't explain it I couldn't even explain it to myself I just felt like be left alone.

When I was in high school I was good at putting on a front with people. I knew people and a lot of people knew me but had no friends. I was the high school flirt. I had a chance to not think about the shit I was facing at home and high school was fun time. I didn't really hang with a crowd of people. Most of the time when I wasn't being a flirt I would be sitting solo. I meet my new boyfriend or shall I say friend. We never had a chance to have sex. Sex never came up in our relationship. He came over to my house a lot after school and we mainly talked. My parents seemed to like him at least they let him come into the house. Well he talked about his mother who was dying soon from lupus and he would talk to me about it. His father was already dating another woman and his mother wasn't even dead yet. And he was upset about it because he didn't know what he was going to do when she passed away. We skipped class a lot to just sit in the back of school and talk sometimes we would sit and hold each other. He was going through bullshit at home and I was dealing with shit that I never shared with him.

One day we were sitting in the back of the school as usual. He puts his hands up my shirt and I freaked out. I can't remember what triggered it but the moment he put his hand up my shirt I turned into another person. He had never done that before and it had been done to me before by my ex boyfriend from the neighborhood and my uncle but today it did not feel right. I can't remember what exactly I told him I know I said something about my uncle having sex with me and then I was crying. The next thing he said "was you need to tell your family I will go with you after school to your house and I will be with you while you tell your family".

On the way home he didn't say anything on the bus ride he just held my hand. We arrived at my house and we got the little orphans off the school bus as usual and we did the homework routine. My mother was at work so she wouldn't be home until after 11 p.m. My dad was gone fishing so he would be home in a couple of hours. I know at this point I wanted to die. I would rather die than face my mother again. I would rather die than hear her complain about me. I would rather die than to have her mad anymore than she has been for the past couple years. She has barely spoken to me in two years and how would I get the courage to tell her what has been going on for years right under her nose. She loved her siblings more than anything more than me. My father called my uncle his son and adored him. My family bragged about his new his military career and his new family he was starting. No one on my mother side of the family has barely made it past high school and if they did they didn't achieve much worth talking about so how can I taint the star of the family. My mother made it to college but couldn't finish her last semester because they ran out of money. She told me that she would go to school hungry because her grandparents only had enough money to send her to school not send her to school and feed her.

I couldn't face her and I knew in my heart I couldn't. I had my boyfriend there he was strong enough to stand with me and not strong enough to protect me against my mother's raft. I decided to try and take my own life that day. I opened a bottle of Tylenol and took all that was in the bottle and I took some of my father's prescription medicine that he had on the table. I remember my boyfriend calling 911 and the 2 little foster girls looking at me scared and crying but I didn't care. I just knew I didn't want to face my mother again. My boyfriend kept screaming at me to stay awake and not close my eyes he was dragging me up and trying to make me walk around the room. I don't remember how long it was I passed out I woke up again I was in the hospital being rushed down the hall then I blacked out again. The next thing I remember was in the "Light". I remember feeling so good and happy I remember walking down the tunnel and I seen my Uncle who passed 2 years earlier and he had told me "it was not my time yet". And after he said that he pushed me and I flew backwards. Then the next thing I remember was someone saying "she's back" and I was in a hospital room with a mask over my face and hooked up to all kinds of stuff. The pearly gates, the light at the end of the tunnel and angels I was now a believer of all of that.

When I was put into a room the first person I seen was my boyfriend he was crying and told me “I am going to kick your ass” we laughed and then he said he loved me and would be back to see me soon. I never saw my parents but I heard my mother cussing up a storm in the hospital hallway the first night I was there. While I was there no one came to visit me. I stayed a few days I can’t remember how many but it was a few. Since I tried to commit suicide they put me in the crazy house for a few days. A counselor came to talk to me. She was white and was tall very tall for a woman. She had short blonde hair. I had to tell her about what happened and why I did that to myself. I told her my uncle was having sex with me and I didn’t know how to tell anyone. She never asked me any details as to where how long this has been going on or what exactly it was that he made me do. But she was writing things down on a tablet and told me that when I was released that she would be assigned to do home visits with me every other day for a few weeks.

When I released to go back home my parents didn’t come get me the counselor took me home instead. When I got there I was greeted by my boyfriend and the 2 little foster girls who are a pain in the ass but at this moment I was glad they were there. They told me how scared they were and I told them I was sorry I didn’t mean to upset them or scare them. My mother put on the biggest front that bitch needed an Oscar. She was very sure not to greet me physically my dad did and then he asked how I was doing. The counselor told them that she would be back the day after tomorrow around 4:00 p.m. to visit with me. My boyfriend stayed a few hours we laughed and talked with the 2 foster girls then he walked home. When we were all alone and the girls were gone to bed I got the cuss out of a life time. Not one time did this selfish ass bitch ask me how did I feel? She proceeded to cuss me out about "now you have the white man all in our business" and "I may lose my foster care license over this shit you pulled". All I could do was stand there and look at her. She never asked me what happened, how long, what he did, or why you never said anything. None of those questions like a normal concerned parent would ask. I felt like Cinderella and she was the evil step mother. She cussed me the hell out. She didn't understand or even ask about the pain and suffering I had been hiding for years. That was of no concern. She was more concerned about "how I am going to make the family look bad if I open my mouth about my uncle". Then she pulls the manipulative move on me "how would your Big Momma feel if she found this out, she would be so hurt you don't want to hurt your Big Momma do you?" Now she knows I love my Big Momma to death and I would never want to hurt her never. "That would make the family look so bad if you say anything tell the people you made it up so they will stop coming bye here and asking questions". I asked her if I could get counseling and she tells me "No just get over it you will be alright". My father says nothing not one word not one question not a thing.

I am alone nowhere to go no one to turn to for help. I don't have a clue as to what to do all I know is to ask God for help. That is what they teach you in church bring all your problems to the altar. I asked him to help me many times and got mad at him because he didn't let me die and let me live instead to just be alone still with no help no relieve. I am still stuck to sit here and be emotionally tortured by my mother.

Its prom time at high school and the counselor is still coming by she asks me questions about my life growing up. She never asked me about my uncle. She just asked me questions like "did you have a fun childhood" or "did you parents whip you". I lie because my mother has already told me to. I please my mother because she already hates me so if lie maybe she will forgive me just a little and go back to how we use to be. Maybe the name calling will stop forever.

My boyfriend is a senior so it's his prom and he asks my dad can I go with him. The prom is in 2 weeks and I have no dress. My dad tells me not to worry he knows a lady that can make me a dress. I just have to show her a picture of the dress I want. I let my boyfriend pick out my dress. We looked in a wedding magazine and he finds one that he likes. I give it to my dad and he takes it to the lady. When he comes back he tells me we are going to go see her tomorrow so she can start making my dress just like the picture. She was an elderly black woman somewhere in here late 80's. She told me she had been sewing all her life. She shows me pictures of the dresses and choir robes she has made in the past. And then she tells she doesn't need a pattern she just needs a picture and the person measurement. I never did learn how to sew my mother was too busy being mad at me to show me how to sew. Now later on when I arrive home the counselor is at the house. I tell her about the prom and we go shopping to pick out the accessories to go with my dress. My mother has nothing to do with prom preparations. The only thing she did was make me a hair appointment. I don't think she even took the day off from work to see me on my prom day.

Prom day was great for him and for me. I had my license but wasn't allowed to drive at night pass 9 o'clock P.M. And he didn't have a license yet so his cousin was our chauffer for the night. We took pictures we danced and laughed. That day we were the shit. I looked good and he looked good. He had gotten him some contacts so he didn't have on his Run DMC glasses that tonight. I liked him with his glasses but without him he was even better looking.

My counselor has stopped coming by to check on me. She told me that my parents told her they didn't need her services anymore and I wouldn't be seeing her. She gives me her card and tells me to call her if I ever wanted to talk. When she was doing her visits we didn't talk much. I knew already to be quiet. I had gotten a stern warning from my mother. Well I didn't call her if though I wanted to call her and tell her the whole story, my mom has cussed so much about me trying to kill myself that I chose to just shut up. "I had to leave work early for this shit" not once did she ever stop to think about how I was doing. If I had the perfect life to the outside world then why would I try to kill myself? Now my uncle was never convicted of any crime because my mother told me to tell the counselor that I lied about everything I said to them when I was in the hospital. I didn't know what else to do so I did. This would not be the last attempt on my life.

A few months went by after prom. My boyfriend mother died and in the same week his dad moves his new girlfriend in the house. My boyfriend is devastated and hurt about it. I listened to him and was there like he was for me but I start getting that same feeling I got with my ex-boyfriend that I don't want to be bothered feeling and I can't explain shit again. So for no particular reason I cut things off with him.

I adjust myself in the arms of my boyfriend as we both look up at the ceiling as he tries to digest all that I have just told him. "That's all I have to say for now" I tell him as I stare at the ceiling until I fall asleep.

Here I am battling feelings of anger within myself. The nice affectionate woman he met has taken a vacation. It has been a couple of weeks since I last talked about my past. Talking about my past has done more harm than good. I feel myself running like I have done in the past. I feel nothing but anger inside of me. I am starting small arguments for no reason with him. Anger spark up between us. But my man has better sense than to give in. He must have had this type of battle before. He doesn't give into my anger he knows the rage I feel was not caused by him. "If you want to talk then talk. If you want to fight then hit yourself. I told you before I don't fight women and I don't like to argue" he says to me while making himself comfortable on the bed. "Come on and sit your ass down and tell me what the hell is wrong with you" he says while patting the bed gesturing me to sit down.

Part 3

How to hide pain

Where did you come from?

You must have escaped from the depths of hell there is no way my
Merciful God would let you out
To come upon me like a thief in the night to ravage me, deceive me,
And rip me up from the inside out
Where did you come from hiding out like a prisoner on the run?
There is no way in hell my precious God would let you out
To come upon me like a butcher ready for the morning slaughter
To gut me open from the inside out
You must have lied your way out of your eternal hell there is no
Way my merciful God would have let you out

I never received any comfort or sympathy from my dad or my mom. They never even asked why I tried to kill myself. I don't know if my dad was hurt because the man he raised from a small boy and trusted as his son had did this unexplainable act of cruelty to his biological daughter or was be hurt because he was so caught up in his drinking that he never noticed what was happening to his own child right in front of him. My mother she manipulated me into feeling low to the point where I blamed myself. She never asked me what happened or what was done. I had no one to tell I didn't even know how to get it off my chest or my mind let alone tell someone how I felt about it. All she did was complained about was "how bad I would make the family look if I said anything" or "just get over it". Or "Everyone down south is going to be talking about Big Momma". How can you get over something that no one wanted to hear? How can you get over something when the monster is discovered and goes through untouched and unpunished? How can you get over it when the people your parents are too ashamed to address what the fuck happened to their own child?

I think I am a smart person. My mother always pushed me to go for the top when it came to school work. I always had good grades in school.

I had received certificates and awards for all my hard work. It's my senior year and I am making college plans. I do what everyone else does. I send out for information on colleges. I want to become a veterinarian. I love animals all kinds it doesn't matter if it's a fish, bird or dog as long as it's not a human I would love it unconditionally. My parents have never discussed anything with me as far as college goes. I just assumed that I would be going they sent my uncle why not me. I am their flesh and blood. My mother hasn't really spoken or dealt with me since my abortion 2 years ago and the suicide attempt didn't make it any better between us. But she acts like a bitch in the house when I'm around rolling her eyes at me or giving me looks of disgust just like she use to give my half sister. But my uncle oh that mother fucker is still calling the house and speaks and talks to my parents and they act like everything is just wonderful and this bastard never did a thing. He hasn't came back to visit the house since I opened my mouth about it. I wonder what he told his new wife. I wonder if she knows exactly what it is she is married to. But my mother still sends him care packages and birthday cards and Christmas gifts her loving feeling for her dear brother has not changed one bit. And I can't even get a hello from her ass without an attitude now that is fucked up. I'm the victim at least that is what I thought.

Anyway I have been scooping out colleges my dreams and hopes are high. My grades are good and I have been lucky enough to have never failed or have to attend summer school. Then one day my mother comes into my room and tells me "You can stop having those college brochures sent here. I am not paying for you to go to those colleges and I am not filling out any financial aide forms or loans for you. If you like you can go to the community college downtown and I will see if I can do that" and walked away. I was hurt beyond belief. My dreams and goals just got snatched away by a bitch who hasn't really spoken to me in two years. I went to my dad and told him what I wanted to do and he said he couldn't do anything about it that is what your mother decided.

My mother made sure her siblings got financial help from her whenever they needed it. If they needed money for college, trade school or to help with some personal bills paid she was right there and they didn't have to ask twice and didn't have to beg. But me no help or comprise. I was hurt but I wouldn't cry. I knew how to ask God for help that is what I was taught in church. I have been going to church all my life with my mother every Sunday like clockwork. But if she was a so called Christian how could you let your own child hurt so much just because of your own pride and ignorance.

I'm 17 now and full of anger. My parents deep down inside know why but pride or embarrassment won't let them address the issue out in open with me. I have already been drinking for years. So now I just do it out in the open. I sit on the front porch with my dad and drink. I'm drinking beer, wine coolers and every now and then I have a shot of liquor. Some of my friends thought it was so cool for me to be 17 and drinking and cussing around my parents. Well mainly my dad because my mom is still working second shift so she can't be bothered. I figured out that was her hiding place second shift. In reality alcohol was the comfort my parents didn't give me. And they didn't stop me from drinking. But after a while anger started to build up. The respect that I had for my parents was slowly leaving me. So cussing while conversating with them became routine for me to say "I don't give a dam" or "this is fucked up" was normal language for me to use when addressing my parents. I did use a lot of foul language towards them every other word that came out of my mouth was foul. My relatives and neighborhood friends seen this as me being a spoil child because my parents never tied to correct me but deep down inside they knew I was lashing out at them. But being the cowards that they were they ignored the issue.

Senior year is almost over with. People are talking about the colleges they are going to attend or the military branch they are going to join. Me I am quiet as a church mouse because right now I can't see past the next day.

One day while looking through the Sunday paper I ran across an ad for the Educational Opportunity Center or E.O.C. There is a listing of all the free trades you can take up there. It wasn't exactly college but it was something. And sometimes little steps help you gain strength when you need to make the big steps later. And plus it was free and my mother can't bitch, complain or whine or even tell me no because it's not costing her a dime.

I graduated from high school and I know I could have done better. Once my mother told me I wasn't going to college I basically said fuck it. She wouldn't even give me money for my PSAT my junior year or my SAT's exams my senior year. And that was something the colleges were asking to see.

My two cousins came up for my graduation it's nice to have them around it gives me a chance to escape reality for a while. They are here for the whole summer of 1990 so my mother is stuck treating me like a daughter again in front of company. Inside I get annoyed with her when I see her play and laugh with them. The second I go over there or try to join in she makes sure not to interact with me. But I know when they leave its back to the same Cinderella treatment.

I meet my oldest son father that summer one day while me and my cousin were walking down the street to get ice cream. He is almost 8 years older than me. He is tall with light skin and green eyes. We exchange numbers and later on I become his girlfriend.

I get accepted into E.O.C and I began taking up classes in September at E.O.C to be a dental assistant. The school hours are the same as if I were in high school. They call me the baby of the class because I am 17 and the other ladies are a lot older than me. After school it's the same routine get the foster kids off the bus and deal with them like you gave birth to them. I'm out of high school at age17. I don't go to parties, clubs or any friend's house. I don't even have friends come over to visit me. Every now and then I go to my boyfriend house on the weekend for a few hours and even then I have to take those foster kids with me if my mom is out working. I have nothing against the kids but I am sick and tired of being bothered with them.

I graduate from E.O.C and receive my state certification as a Dental Assistant. Things didn't work out as I thought. I was unable to find a job as a dental assistant but the knowledge is priceless. I signed up to take up a personal care aide classes and do that for a living for a while. Later on about 2 years later I did go back to E.O.C to become a certified nurse assistant.

I am still living at home and one day I got into it with my mother about something I really can't remember what it was. I'm 18 now and being a babysitter is getting on my nerves. I leave home and move in with my boyfriends friend after me and my mother have that argument. I don't talk to my parents for a few years after that. I became pregnant at 21 with my first son. My boyfriend goes and tells my parents I am pregnant because I wasn't speaking to them at the time. And I wasn't going to form a relationship again with them because I am pregnant. And to my mother it would probably give her something to scream about. "Your back now because your pregnant" I would eat dirt before I let her make me feel like shit again. I had no intention of telling them anything about it. And because of my boyfriend and my dad I started to develop a talking relationship again with my mother around the 5th month of my pregnancy. We had moved 2 blocks away from my parent's house. So I began to walk over there when I got off of work mainly to talk to my father for a little while. But by this time my mother was out on leave because she had injured her back at work. She would give me dirty looks when I would go over there. But inside I had missed my father so I bit my tongue in order to keep my relationship with him alive.

My first son is born finally after 3 days of labor February 14th at 7:30 p.m. He came into the world at 9 pounds and 3 ounces. My mother and my boyfriend were there with me the whole time eating chicken wings while I was in agony eating ice chips. He was the most beautiful thing I had ever seen his hair well that was nappy he came into the world needing a perm but that was okay he was mine and I promised him no one would ever hurt him as long as I was breathing. But now that I look back at his baby picture my God he was a weird looking thing not anything to write home about. But at that moment in my eyes he was the prettiest thing ever created.

My parents are very happy with the birth of their first grandchild especially my dad. My dad and his brother came to see me when I was in the hospital. They took pictures of him and all said "where did that nappy ass hair come from". Maybe my mother is happy because my cousin had a baby

2 months before me. She was so happy that my cousin had a baby she was so happy for her sister who was now a grandmother. If I had my child first I probably would have received the "you're going to embarrass the family speech". But my parents are happy and they spoiled their first grandchild to death.

My relationship with my son dad is normal to a certain point. We go out together and we hang with friends. We have family dinners with his family members on a regular. But I never shared my past with my uncle with him. I basically went to move in with him to get away from my parents not for love. I wanted out of my nightmare and he helped me get out. But I was still in a nightmare not physically but mentally and emotionally I was fucked up and I just didn't know it. We had sex like normal people nothing was ever forced or demanded. But I always wanted to have it in the dark. I never wanted him to see my body and in a way I didn't want to see his either. He never thought it was strange whenever I was in the room changing I would always hurry up and cover myself and he would joke and say "I saw it before" but I still wanted to cover myself. If when looking at him it would remind me of my uncle and it was hard having sex with one man your boyfriend but to have visions of a monster in your head. That is the hardest thing I had to deal with learning how to enjoy sex inside. It's easy to have sex and then roll to your side of the bed and hide whatever it was you were feeling. But I always covered up my body I never walked around naked I front of him. A part of me hated my body. I hated being this pretty woman everyone else saw. I hated dressing up and I just hid all my pain behind a fake smile and played it off like I was shy. And my temper well towards men it was unpredictable and at time uncontrollable when I lost it. I not only scared myself but those around me feared me when I got mad.

The relationship came to an end after almost 1 year after the birth of my first son. He was seeing someone else an old girlfriend of his. We were also engaged so the ultimate act of betrayal. It just added more reason for me not to trust people especially men. When I first found out I was pregnant with our son he went and proposed to me and gave a small diamond ring. But rumor has it that he was at an ex-girlfriend house and her boyfriend or husband showed up at house while he was there. I guess that is how he ended up getting shot. But instead of telling the truth he told his family I had a boyfriend shot him. He forgot to tell his family that I found out about the other woman and found a copy of a birth certificate of a child he fathered while we were together. This caused me to move out of the apartment 3 weeks prior to him getting shot. Not only did his family take his side of the story and cut me off but they also cut off my son. When I did find out about him cheating on me I moved back in with my family. I told my parents what I had found out and they told me to just leave him and come back home until I could get my own apartment. I was shocked because this was my mother telling me it was okay to move back home. "Just leave everything" she told me. I left everything. I grabbed my clothes and everything that was in my son nursery. But I couldn't tolerate my mother tolerating me even thou she worked 2nd shift. I knew they were still into foster care and needed me to be the babysitter again.

I felt nothing but anger and resentment whenever I was around her. I tried so hard to love her because she is my mother. It's like its okay to treat me like shit I still love you mommy. But for her to love me back as her child it's not going to happen. She does things out of routine or obligation not love. It's routine for someone to give you a birthday card doesn't mean they really mean the words in the card. It's an obligation to some to give your child shelter if they lose their own shelter it doesn't mean you really want to help them.

One day while I am there my uncle calls the house and I answered the phone and handed it to her. She has a conversation with him asking about how he is doing and how his kids and wife were doing. And at the end of the conversation she fucked up and told that mother fucker she loved him in front of me. I went the fuck off. I cussed her out and my dad out. I had never cussed them out before this was the first time and won't be the last. I started breaking shit and threatening to kill them all. I grabbed a knife from the kitchen and I started cutting up the furniture in the living room. My dad kept saying" I did do something I did" and I just keep asking "what did you do to him" I never got an answer. My mom ran into the kitchen and called 911 on me and the police came and threw me out the house. So after that fall out I ended up moving around the corner with a friend for about 2 weeks then to my own apartment. Later on that year I replaced the furniture that I destroyed. But parents feared me from that day on. They got a taste of just how much anger was inside of me.

I can't comprehend in my mind how my mother could love the monster and not have sympathy for the victim her only child. She showed him more compassion than she ever showed me. Days like that use to make me wish I was dead because the pain I felt inside was unexplainable. My dad I was mad at him but not as much as my mother. As a father I felt he should have done a lot more than he did even thou he never explained to me what he did. But my mom still loved her brother and my father still claimed him as his son. But my father still told me he loved me he never stop using those words every day of his life rather I was talking to him or not he made it his business to tell me that. Even when I left home at the age of 18 he drove by my apartment every day I would see him drive pass. And our eyes would meet and we would have that silent communication. He still hugged me and kissed like he did from the time I was born and never stopped loving me. I just couldn't and can't understand why my mother hated me so much over something I had no control over.

I have my own apartment, my son, a job and a car my dad brought for me. No friends or family to visit or chat with I am pretty much a loner. My first baby daddy is dead beat to the bone. The Court ordered him to pay $5.25 a week in child support he won't even do that. He fought me for visitation rights that he never used. One day I asked him for help. To help me buy his son some clothes he replies "I'm not fucking you; you better go ask that mother fucker you with to help you". Those fucked up words he said to me did nothing but give me strength. It hurt that a man would not help his own child but it also made me stronger. Some men think that just because you have a child by them that they are still entitled to sleep with you still even after they have moved on with someone else. And when you don't sleep with them they take it out on the child. But I knew that after that day that I would never ask another person again for help and pray that God would make it so that I don't have to depend on no one but him.

I met my second baby daddy after I had moved into my apartment he was one my neighbors. We had sex one day for the first time and I got pregnant. I think it was around Valentine day. I wasn't seeing anyone and he wasn't seeing anyone. He asked me if I wanted company and I said yeah and one thing lead to another. I didn't tell my parents about my new pregnancy. I had moved out of their house and we weren't exactly on speaking terms. But I did share the information with my cousin she was also pregnant with her second child at the time. Then one day I was at the doctor office getting a prenatal check up and I had my oldest son with me he was around 4. Some kind of way I went into a seizure while sitting in the waiting room. I remember when I woke up sometime during the next day and the nurse told me I went into a seizure while sitting in the waiting room. They had contacted my parents since they were listed in my film as emergency contacts. I had been out of it for almost 12 hours. I had to stay in the hospital for almost a month because I kept going into seizure and I would black out for hours. And by me being pregnant it wasn't safe for me or the baby to leave. I begin asking the nurse were my son was and she told me" your parents came and got him after we called them to inform them that you went into a seizure". I remember talking to my dad on the phone and he told me that my son was okay he was safe and just get better. I was about 5 months pregnant at the time and this incident caused me and my parents to start a speaking relationship again.

When I was released from the hospital I called my parents house and told them to drop off my son. I was big as a house during this pregnancy. By the time I was 6 months I was unable to reach my gas pedal for my car. My dad was glad to have me back into life. He had his grandson around again and me. Me and my mother's relationship is still the same. I know she is faking I can see right through her. She is good at putting on a good ass front for my father and his brother. She is being a good actress for her sister and her neighbors. Talking about how happy she is about being a grandmother and then rolling her eyes at me all in the same breath.

She invites me and my son to go church with her and the foster children she now has. And even thou we are at church worshipping God together I know in my heart that my mother's delight for me being back around is just a front. Like I said before actions speak louder than words. I remember one time we were at church and we had to hold hands for prayer and at this particular occasion I just happen to be sitting next to her so she had to hold my hand. But instead of holding my hand she grabs one of the foster children that was in her care and places them in between us so she wouldn't have to hold my hand. That action right there just secured the feeling I was feeling all along that she was being a fake even in the house of the Lord.

My second son arrived four weeks early. I went into labor on Halloween and they hospitalized me until the doctor knew everything was okay with him because of the seizures. But I read all the side effects the medicine could have on your baby so I refused to take the medicine and just prayed that I would make it through this pregnancy okay. So after about a week of being in and out of labor he arrives in the world in November around 1:15 p.m. at 9 pounds and 15 ounces and 4 weeks early. He was the ugliest baby I have ever seen in my life. I remember saying that after I gave birth to him in the delivery room to his father. He was so mad at me he started going off saying "he is not ugly". But he was I am his mother and I was being honest. The first 2 months of his life he was a little on the ugly side then when he was about 3 months old he started to get cute.

My mom doesn't talk shit about me having a second child because her favorite niece is also pregnant with her second baby. So I guess again this isn't an act of embarrassment. If I was an embarrassment then what would her niece be? But I did get the "both of her kids have the same father" comment a few time whenever she could throw it in. But her mother which is my Big Momma has 10 kids and each have a different daddy! Is her own mother an embarrassment in her eyes?

My second son is around 5 months old and my first son is somewhere near 5. And my second son father decides he want to kill us. He called me one day right before I left work and told me he was going to "kill us" and hangs up the phone. I guess the stress of being a father is getting to him I really don't know. We had never had any problems or arguments before or after the birth of our son. He is about 4 years younger than me. He was making plans to go to college and I guess having to work a part time job and take care of his son was too much for him to bare. I took care of 80% of the household expenses. I worked a full time job and went to college full time also. I guess women can handle more than men. So then one day he snaps no warning no anything. Just calls me at work and says he is going to "kill us". It was like some shit off of television or some story that you hear about in the news. I had one of the little orphans be a baby sitter for me and I knew she was on her way to my house.

So I left work early to hurry up and pick up the babies from daycare. She would come and watch my children from 5 p.m. to 8 p.m. while I took up classes at college at night. I told him he could go to college around his part time work schedule it was not the end of the world. He was saying he wanted to go to college in Atlanta and I told him fine go I don't have a problem with that. Like I said he calls me and tells me he was going to kill me and the children and hang up the phone. I drove as fast as I could to go get the kids from daycare but he had already picked them up which was something he had never done before so I panic and drive back home. By this time one of the foster girls my mom use to take care of was already at my house with her girlfriend and they were waiting on me to let them in the house. She asked me what was wrong I explained to her what had happened and what he had said to me. I panic because I don't know where he is at or what he is driving he didn't own a car. I had nothing to tell the police right then so I didn't call them. Then he shows up about 20 minutes after I arrived home. I opened the door and there he was with the children. He pushed me back into the apartment. He then let go of my oldest son arm and my son runs to the baby sitter. I ask him to give me the baby. Instead he threw him across the room. My little baby hit the wall all I heard was a 'thump" no screams, cries or noise. At that very moment I just knew he was dead. The baby sitter ran and grabbed a broom out of the kitchen. She was only 14 but she tried to defend us. I seen him going towards her so instead I started hitting him so he wouldn't jump on her. I screamed to her to take my son and run. I laid on top of my baby while he beat the fuck out of me. I can't remember what all he was saying to me while he beating my ass I just laid there with my son underneath me not knowing if he was dead or alive. The police finally arrived and got him off of me. Me and my son were taken to an area hospital and treated and released within a few hours. I drove by his family house on the way home and explained to his uncle and his mother what he had done. His uncle said "he has really fucked up now" and his mother just stood there staring at me like I was crazy. I showed her the police report and she looked it over. She gave it back to me and I got back into my car and went home. At the time I was working for a preschool and I didn't go to work for a few weeks. My face was messed up and I didn't want the children or my co-workers asking me questions about what happened. I looked like the elephant man little sister or daughter just pick one. But I still attended college people looked at me in class but they didn't ask or say anything to me about my face. My son had to get testing done on him every month for about 2 years because they thought he may have had brain damage from getting thrown into the wall at a young age. My second son father went to jail for a few weeks and then we had to go to court. I could not believe his dam family supported him and defended him. Talking about he was just stressed about at being a new father he was around 22 years of age at the time. Man give me a fucking break. But then again this is just how some families have monsters in them and they then continue to hide the monster just like my parents hid my uncle. So after we went to court the judge issued me and my parents a restraining order. My parent received one theirs did not have an expiration date. And I received a restraining order for five years and then after that I had to go and get it renewed every five years. I cut all ties off with him and his family there was no way I could forgive them for defending his actions not only towards me but towards my son also. I never spoke to him or his family for about 10 years. When my son got old enough to ask me about where his dad was at or why he has never seen his dad. I showed him the police report and court papers explaining to him the reason his dad and his family were not in his life. It would be about 10 years before I talk to my second son dad after that incident.

My son met his father for the first time 10 years later. He looks a lot like him but I pray he will be a better man than him. I went and filed for child support because I was receiving day care assistance and for me to continue receiving it I had to file for child support. After I file we had to see each other for the first time in almost 10 years. There wasn't anything to say to him so during the court procedure we came up with a visitation agreement. He also agreed to pay $65.00 a week for child support which he never continued to pay. He came with the same bull shit my oldest son father did telling my son "I am going to be in your life, I miss you, I love you".

He made a one- time child support payment and that was because he had a family reunion that was happening a week after our court date. So to keep me from being and telling him my son couldn't go with him he hurried and made the first child support payment and the last. Now he took my son to the family reunion for show off reasons nothing more. How can you brag about our son after what you did and not being in his life for the first 10 years of it? Yes I had a restraining order against him but I never barred his mother or grandmother from seeing him. They were upset that I had him put in jail. After the family reunion I never received another child support payment and my son never received another visit from him or his family and they lived on the next block less than a 5 minute walk from my house. My son was very hurt. But I reminded him "we have done fine without him during the first 10 years of your life and we will continue to do better without for the rest of your life". My son is a beast on the football field we would see his dam father at the football games only when we played against his girlfriend son team. Like a dead beat dad he said "I will come see you play at your games". I remember for the first 3 games my son was so excited he would look all over the field for his father. Wanting what a son wants and that is to show off for his dad. But he never came to see him play. My son was so hurt he use to cry I heard him tell his father when and where he was playing at but he never came. That fucked my son head up. How could you with this other chick make time to watch her son play football and not your own son? I was willing to turn the other cheek about what he had done for the sake of my son but when you are forgiven and then you turn around and still continue to fuck up either I am stupid or a dam fool. And I told my son "what don't kill you makes you stronger. I'm here so fuck him and fuck him hard". After me explaining what he did to him as a baby my son still had love for him you would think the stupid mother fucker would take advantage of his son love for him but he didn't. His lost is all I can say.

My third son was born 18 months after my second son. This was not suppose to happen. I was getting the depo shot every 3 months like clockwork. But I had a throat infection and my tonsil was messed up and they had to put me on anti-bodics. I did not know and my doctor did not tell me 'hey fool use a condom antibiotics keep your birth control from working" so again trial and error.

So one day my evening classes at college were cancelled due to the bad weather. I decided not to call my man and go home early to surprise him and get it in. Since I have been busy with work and school we really didn't have time for one another during the week. So I get home and this mother fucker got a white chick in my bed. He told her I was his cousin and that he was watching the kids while I went to school. I grabbed my metal baseball bat and went to swinging they ran out of house but ass naked in the god dam snow. He calls me about 2 hours later saying he wanted his clothes and his car keys. I said okay come by and get them. I took the car keys drove his car in the middle of the empty field that was next door packed all his shit inside of it and lit the shit on fire. Went to the corner store got me a 40 ounce beer sat on the porch and enjoyed watching the shit burn. Then took his furniture that was in the apartment and threw it off the top balcony and let is smash to the ground into a thousand pieces. He came by seen his stuff broken and burning and just turned around and left.

Now I go to the doctor the following month to get my depo shot. And that is when I discovered I was pregnant with my third son. I was mad very mad because I have just broken up with this fool there is no way to fix the relationship and I am stuck with another child. I told my cousin and I told my ex-boyfriend mother because we worked together that I was pregnant. I did not share this information with my parents just yet. I was almost finished with school and I had about 6 months left until I was done. I hid the pregnancy almost to the very day I was due. It was Memorial Day and we were in the backyard at my parent's house and my dad says to me "so when were you going to tell us you were pregnant." I didn't say a word I just had this fucked up look on my face. Then he says "well when is the baby due" and I said "next weekend". My father started screaming "you weren't going to say anything just sit here and have a baby next week". Then my mother had to jump in and get her two cents in "you have two kids at least your cousin lives with her boyfriend and her kids have the same father you have 3 kids now and they have different fathers and they don't do shit for those kids". I just sat there didn't bother to go into details about how I became pregnant. I thought I wasn't going to get pregnant because I was on the Depo shot but one mistake changed that and it wasn't worth defending myself over. So I turned and looked at her and asked her "would you have liked it better if I had an abortion" and turned around and continued to take her verbal abuse because those ribs were to dam good to stop eating that day.

My son came just a little early. The funny thing was my Big Momma was in town at the time and I had brought us some wrestling tickets. She is a big WWF fan and so I thought it would be fun to take her. We enjoyed dinner at a Chinese buffet that I took her to. Now to this day I can never figure out how my Big Momma wearing some skin tight red jeans on sitting at the same table with me and steal about 50 chicken wings. We were at the wrestling match and I asked her did she want something to eat and she said no. Then she started pulling out all these chicken wings out of her pants pocket. It was the funniest thing ever we still laugh about it today because she didn't have a purse but her pockets were full of chicken wings. The same day I was suppose to graduate from college I was having him. So instead of walking across the stage I was having him in a delivery room. Oh well we can't have everything at the same time. It was around 9:15 a.m. on a June morning. He came into the world at 7 pounds 13 ounces had I not been trying to hide him he probably would have gotten up to 9 pounds like his brothers. My mother other relatives were also there from out of town. Her favorite sister, my two cousins and my cousin 2 kids and my big momma. I went to stay at my parent's house after I was released from the hospital. I guess I was trying to act social around family and plus everyone were there visiting I may as well stay over there to. Now one day my relatives wanted to go to Niagara Falls and I wanted to drive my father new van he asked if I would drive them and I said yes. Then I guess he decided I wasn't mature enough and said he wanted my cousin to drive instead. So I acted like a bitch threw a tantrum and left the house. But that wasn't the issue the issue was I didn't want to be around them. The love my mother showed them made me sick and angry. And I couldn't stand it so I was looking for a reason to snap to get away from it.

My youngest son has never seen his dad or any of his father's relatives. His mother who was a co-worker of mine only seen him once when he was first born and that was because I took him up to my job after I had given birth to him. I did take his father to court for child support. He did truck driving for a local meat company. I use to get payments here and there or whenever they caught up with him. He made the promise in court "I want to be a part of my son life" bull shit and more bull shit I heard the same words before just out of another mouth. I approached his mother one day while at work just before I left there to start another job I think my son was about 3 months old. I ask her did she want my son to come over and visit them. She tells me "I can't accept that child because you and my son had him out of wed lock". People kill me when they try to use religion as a way to justify their actions. That was fine because I was not going to beg or cry over spilled milk. She never told our co-workers that my son was her grand child and I never mentioned it either. Fuck her and him life goes on at the end of the day it's all on me and I am leaning on God.

What do you do for money when you have 3 kids of your own and 2 little orphans staying with you? Well you have a few option 1- get another job 2- go to school and try to get a better paying job 3- sell drugs doesn't matter if you're a woman 4- rob a bank or rob someone 5- pawn all of your valuables if you have any or 6 – sell some ass to an old man with a social security check. I tired option 1 and 2 didn't quite work out at the time. Couldn't try option 5 because I didn't have anything worth taking to the pawn shop. Now option 6 it was good for a while. I found an old man with a social security check and couldn't have sex which was even better. He found simple pleasure in watching me clean his house up naked. Back then I was 140 pounds size 10 couldn't tell me my body wasn't worth looking at. So once a week I would clean his house. And accompany him on his little gambling trips to the casinos. I even had access to his car when I wanted to drive it. After a year of being his naked maid he found someone more close to his age to marry. Which was something we both agreed needed to be done he was lonely and I sure as hell couldn't be his woman like that. But even after he gotten married he still found a way to give me money every now and then. I guess he was paying for old memories.

So now my little sugar daddy is gone and it time to think up another way to keep the household a float. How can you rob someone and not go to jail for it? Well white men are some funny little creatures. Sometimes I sit back and laugh at them. Especially the high society ones those are mainly the ones who desire a black woman in the back of their minds or are gay behind closed doors or even into some crazy shit that no one else can get into but them. So me and one of my little orphans who were now in her late teens decided to go on the internet and sign up and open up profiles on these date sites using fake pictures or sometimes no pictures at all just good conversation in the chat rooms. We would go into a few chat rooms tell these crazy ass white men what they wanted to hear. It was fun we got a few laughs out of it. Even had a few fools wire us some money. Then there were a few victims. Some of these men all white of course would agree to meet up at little hole in the wall hotels. We would get them all excited and worked them all up then out pops a second person or even a third person and pow they get robbed. They can't tell anyone. How would you explain your reasons for being at a cheap hotel on the other side of town? Doctors, lawyers and a few executives all white and all happily married but willing to take a chance to be with the most desirable thing on earth a colored woman. We did this routine off and on again for a few years and even now we sit back and laugh about our little victims of white society.

Drugs now that is option #3. What a life for people in the hood no education needed but you can't go out there blind you have to think about what it is your doing. Sometimes there isn't a chance to stop or get out. Most of our black men probably around 75% of them have some type of relationship with drugs either they sell it or use it. But what do black folks do when they get more than 2 pennies in their pockets? They showboat of course. Bring all the attention you can get to yourself is a major no no. They have a $50,000 car or truck and no job not even a part time job to make it look legit. You cannot ride around in society for too long with no job but looking like a million bucks. Someone is going to get curious either your neighbors or law enforcement.

I had a friend who didn't have a problem supplying me with weed. I know I wasn't about to stand on no corner selling nickel and dime bags. So my customers were white society people. The ones who talks about how bad drugs are and how dangerous the hood is. Those mother fuckers be smoking more weed than Cheech and Chong. All you need are a few regular customers like that. They don't want attention and you don't want attention. And they aren't buying no nickel and dime bags more like a pound or more. Once a month or once every 2 weeks you make one sale and you're done until next time. I didn't show boat. My agenda was to make sure my bills were paid and everyone was feed and clothed. I keep a broken down van but I had food to eat and enough to share. All my bills were paid on time everyone had clothes had a little money in the bank I even broke my parents off a little something every now and then. I did just enough to keep my household comfortable and enough so I didn't have to ask my dead beat baby daddies for shit.

Now when your ass is doing something you know you're not suppose to be doing the best thing to do is keep it to yourself and keep it as low key as possible. No one has to know how you got this and that. Hell just tell them "I work for it". The only people that need to know are those involved and make sure you deal with people who know how to keep their mouths shut. You don't have to explain to your parents or your kids or even your best friend. Just do what you have to and pray you don't get caught. I was in relationships and the dudes didn't know what I was doing because to me it was none of their business. This little routine was off and on again for a few years. But one of my little orphan sisters stayed in the game for a while. One day her biological brother was mad he was complaining about her moving in on his territory and making sells on his block. During this time I had been out of the game for a few months me and her wasn't talking to one another during this time. I don't know exactly what happened when she went over to his house but the outcome was him ending up dead and her not serving one day in jail for the crime. I guess to the police saw it was a menace to society gone. She had a lawyer that cost $10,000 and he made dam sure she never spent 1 day in jail for that crime. She screamed self defensive she said he reached for the gun on the table but she beat him to it and emptied a few rounds in his chest. Some people on the street say she snitched on a few people made a plea deal and got off. I do know a lot of people in the game kept their distance from her after the incident. Especially when she got off Scott free didn't serve one hour in jail. By this time she had found all of biological sibling and they decided to cut her off completely when she killed her biological brother. That's the game for you if you stay in to long you either go to jail or end up dead. Some people get use to the money involved in the game but sometimes you have to know when to walk away and not go back to it. That's why I kept low key and never announced what I did never said anything about what I did. Someone will kill you just to get your good paying customer and get a few more dollars in their pockets. My little orphans knew what I did and they knew to be quite about it. One day one of them and a friend of theirs wanted to smoke some weed. Me and my friend Danny had a kitchen table full of weed and I was helping him bag it up. They decided to sneak some. So okay you two want to smoke weed let's see you smoke some weed. Danny rolled up some blut's for them and we had them smoke it up. When they got through they never wanted to smoke again. I still tease her about it now. One thing about drugs you can't make money if you're a user.

Now I started dating this guy around the time my youngest son was around 2 years old. There were red flags all over the place that dude was seeing more than just me. My parents seen them but instead of guiding me or talking to me about it they waited until the shit blew up in my face to tell me "I knew that mother fucker wasn't shit" if you knew so much why the hell didn't you tell me or at least put a bug in my ear. So like I said I am dating this guy for a while and one day this woman comes to my house and asks me was I seeing him. And I said yes and she said "well I am seeing him also and he was with me yesterday at the hospital because I had just had a miscarriage." So I am shocked as hell I didn't go off the chain she was respectable so things were cool. Then she goes on to say "I did a little following of him. I followed him for a week or so and these are all the addresses of the women he has been seeing there are a total of 5 women including me and the lady at the door". So I am still in shock I don't know what to say to her. Then she continues to say 'I know where he is right now do you want to go see for you own eyes". I said yes we jump in her car and drive over to this woman house that only lived less than 5 minutes from my house. The house had a big picture window up front and she doesn't have any curtains up so you can basically see right through the house. So I get out of the car go in the drive way see his car in the drive way I flatten all 4 tires. We then go up on the porch they are sitting on the couch in the house so they don't see us standing on the porch looking through the window looking at them. He turns around see's us on the porch I took a brick and threw it through the window the whole window shattered. Me and the lady get back in the car and go back to my house. And can't run out and jump in his the car and come after us because his car is on 4 flats. I get home crying and upset tell her thank you for everything and she drives off I never see her again. I go into the house sad hurt and fucked up. I had gotten so tired of trusting people and needing someone just to get shitted on every dam time. My mother was the starter of it and since then I have always felt alone. Just looking and begging and trusting people just to find out everything was a lie. So to escape the pain I slit my wrist. I had 3 kids at the time but I was tired of hurting and being hurt and I wanted it to end it so I slit my wrist. I don't know if God was looking out for me but dude showed up at my house on 4 flats and seen me on the bathroom floor and rushed me to the hospital on 4 flats. When I woke up the doctors said if I would have cut it another 2 centimeter to the right I would be dead right away. But where I slit it at I lost a lot of blood before he got there which caused me to pass out. I remember standing there watching the blood run out of my arm then passing out and waking up on a hospital table getting stitched up. But I also remembered while I was out going down the tunnel again. The same long dark tunnel I had went down years ago. And I just floated down the tunnel and there I seen the pearly gate and two angels standing there. I remember fighting with them and telling them to let me in. I was tired and I wanted to go to heaven I wanted to be behind that gate. And the one angel pushed me back through the tunnel and the next thing I remember was a nurse standing over me opening up my eye lids telling the doctor I was back. I look at my stitch marks all the time try to remember that no matter how much I hurt it's not that serious. Easier said than done because this won't be the last time.

After I was stitch up I was sent home from the hospital he drove me home and said he would be back later on to talk to me. I was tired from the medicine they gave me and I just wanted to sleep so I didn't put up a fight or argue with him. One of the foster girls that my mother use to take care of was living with me at the time. Yes one of the little orphans. She helped me take all his clothes out of my closet and we threw them all out in the middle of the front yard and I poured bleach all over his clothes. So when he called me I said come get your stuff and when he pulled up he saw all his shit in the yard with bleach on it. I know it was probably ghetto or childish but I wasn't going to let it go that easy even if he did save my life. He had nice suits at my house because he use to work at a funeral parlor. I ran into him a few times after that I even ran up to him and slapped him in the face twice when he was getting gas at the gas station. But I couldn't blame anyone but myself I caused myself all this pain just because I had the need to have someone around me for security. Maybe if I was looking for something more than security I wouldn't have gotten hurt so many times.

Well after that split up one of my little orphan sisters that was staying with me got employed at a pizza shop in the neighborhood. Now it was prom season and she wanted to go to a senior's night out at her high school. Her boss said she could not have the night off because his shop was busy on the weekend. She was upset that she couldn't get the night off. So I came up with an idea. I told her to call off from work because she was sick. Well she did and he called her back and said she was fired. I told her not to worry about it go ahead and you will have your job back tomorrow. Now the next thing I did was get up and I take her to work. I had an old neck brace in the basement I put it on her. I got my recent emergency room receipt and off we went to her job. Her boss saw us when we walked in the door and started yelling "I fired you yesterday get out of here". So now I go into defensive mother mode. "We were in a car accident yesterday you see she is wearing a neck brace" I said to him. "How could she come to work if she is in the emergency room" I asked him. "Here is her receipt from the emergency room right here" I said as I was waving the pink paper in the air but I wouldn't let him read it. You could clearly see the area hospital name on it and you could see there was some kind of writing on it but I wouldn't let him hold it. I just waved it in the air and made my case. He had no choice but to give her back her job. She and I were acting a fool and she was sitting there crying and then we had the customers that were there on our side. Me and her still laugh about that today and how she had to wear that neck brace for two-weeks to go along with the story I made up.

I started a new job at a bank after finishing college the first time I was able to find a better paying job to help take care of me and my boys. I purchased my first home by myself on top of being a single mother of 3. It wasn't a fancy house it was a H.U.D. it was a house that was in foreclosure and was going for cheap. It had what I was looking for at the time 4 bedrooms, 2 bath rooms, a backyard and was in a nice neighborhood. I ended up getting the house for $20,000. Then while I was working at the bank I decided to go back to college for a second time to receive another degree. If I wanted to make more money I need a degree in something else that would make me some money. The one that I had was in computer technology but I was working at a bank and working with numbers was where the money was at.

I started dating my co-worker from the bank son. She told me he was around my age and single and was a great guy and an ex-marine. We were the same age and he had a job at a bakery that was close to my house. We dated for about 3 months until we decided to live together. He wasn't cute at all. He was dark very dark with thick ass Run-DMC glasses. He was medium built always had a low hair cut because he had a residing hair line thing going on. My parents loved him to death he was the only boyfriend that I dated that they actually liked. The boys loved him but I did not love him. I was with him because I didn't want to be alone. I still had the need to have someone in my life I still needed that security from someone. But we got along pretty good. We never had an argument or a disagreement which was something very rare with me. Then for his birthday I brought him some very expensive up to date glasses. They made him look a lot better almost half ass cute. Then one day they came up missing and he was back to wearing his thick as run-DMC glasses again. I asked him about it and he said he left him at his brother house on the other side of town and when he gets a chance he will go over there and get them. Since he did not drive and I was the one he dropped him off at his brother house. So I never thought about it again. Then a few months go by and its Christmas time and I brought him a gold bracelet and after a while that ended up missing in action also. He said that he broke it at work and he put it in the shop to get fixed. Now in the year that we dated, I never had a reason to not trust him. He got paid every Friday and he always gave me my money off the top. Then he would go hang out with his co-workers for a while for a few drinks he said. He never asked me for anything and our sex life was very boring. And I didn't mind that because I didn't feel like being touched anyway. We may have had sex once a week if that I can almost count the times on one hand. When we went to bed it was what it was bed time. There wasn't a lot of intimacy between us. We talked we laughed we joked we went out together but there wasn't a lot of intimacy between us.

Then one day a friend of his popped up at my door. I was shocked because he wasn't home and he told me that he was going to hang out with the friend that was now at my door. So he says "there is something you need to know". And I said "What" he goes well "I know you're a good person you're your man is a crack head". I said "what he can't be." Then he goes on to tell me "he does it every day on his lunch break the glasses and the bracelet you brought him he traded them in for crack. If you come with me now I will take you to the crack house so you can see with your own eyes." I got my purse and key and we got into my van and drove about 4 blocks over to a neighborhood crack house. We got out of the van and walked into the house and there he was high as a kite. I was devastated at what I seen. I remember him saying he was "sorry but I can' t help it" then he told me how he does it every day on his lunch break and how he walks over to the crack house to get a quick fix sometimes when he tells me he is walking to the store to get a beer. I was in total shock. Then one of the little orphans is there with her man at the crack house which he owns. She was selling crack to him the whole time and never said anything to me about it never even gave me a hint of what he was doing behind my back. She just sat in the corner puffing on a blunt with her man laughing at how he finally got busted. I begged him to get help. I told him his job had a program were they pay for you to go to detox for 30 days. He replay was "I don't want the white people at work all in my business." So then I suggested that he could go to the Veteran Administration Hospital and get into drug rehab through them. But he wouldn't do it. The last thing I wanted to do was break up my stable home. Everyone in the family loved and liked him even if I didn't love him. But I had to think about the long haul. Crack heads will steal the sweet out of sugar and sell it for a crack rock. I was very lucky that he didn't steal from me or my kids. Drug addicts don't care what they do or who they hurt to get high. I went back home packed up all his things and took them to the crack house. I pleaded one last time for him to get help so we could keep the family we had made together. I didn't want to bring another man in my boy's life or start the dating thing all over again. But in the end crack won the battle. I left his things all 8 garbage bags on the porch of the crack house at the corner of East Delevan and Newburg and walked away.

I saw his mother that Monday at work. She had already known what had happened over the weekend I guess he may have told her. Her reply was "I knew he was a crack head I just didn't want to say anything. I knew sooner or later you would find out. I got tired of him stealing from me to get crack". Wow was all I could say. We were friends for 3 years she bragged about how nice her son was but forgot to mention "he's a crack head". When people secretly hate on you they think of all kinds of ways to fuck up your life. She hooked me up with a her crack head son while pretending to be my friend because she was tired of him stealing from her what type of friend is that? Then one my little orphan sister was selling crack to him. Yet they both smiled in my face on a regular while waiting for the shit to hit the fan. After that me and her friendship was history I never spoke to her again. And as for my little orphan sister my trust for her went out the door. I had her back no longer and I fed her with a long handled spoon.

I ran into him a few times after this incident. The place he worked for it closed up so he lost his job and because he couldn't stay clean he never found work anywhere else. He looked like shit the times I did see him. He asked how the boys were doing and how my parents were. He knew that he could never come back into my life because crack had taken him over and consumed him. His drug addiction was starting to show. His outfit consisted of dirty clothing and busted up sneakers on his feet. He went from driving a car to riding a bike around town all to get a piece of crack rock. Then the last time I seen him which was about 5 years later he was pushing a grocery cart around neighborhood and picking up soda bottles to cash in for money. All I could do was shake my head and walk away.

But I am not really into anyone at this time in my life. It's been almost a year since I broke up with dude. And I still have a problem with men touching me. I have sex with men because it is natural. And it's like once we do that I turn against them in some sort of way so they won't come back. Once I get that feeling I don't want anything for them anymore. I even had a few out burst with a few guys. We would be having sex and then all of a sudden I would bug out and tell them to get the "fuck out of my house", "or get the hell off of me" or just stop talking to them all together. I wanted to be touched and I wanted some affection but it couldn't be from a man. Having a man touch me was starting to disgusted me so I turned to women. This was a part of my life I kept secret from my family. This was just between me and the female I was with. I didn't have friends that were close to me like that to even know what I was in a relationship with a woman. So I start a relationship with a woman that I worked with at the bank. It wasn't just about sex I just wanted to enjoy having some hold me without the feeling of being violated. And without feeling disgusted after we touched. I know a man can do this and that but in my case a man wasn't doing nothing but building more anger up inside of me every time one touched me.

So I know this is not the normal thing according to the Bible and trying to deal with this on my own is very hard. Her presence gives me peace. I think because I wanted that mother nurturing after the secret about my uncle came out and I didn't get it. So now I have it. I enjoyed laying in her arms. And she did not try to turn me out and turn me against men. Some studs take advantage of women that they encounter who are victims of abuse. Me turning into a lesbian wasn't going to heal me it was just going to bury the pain a little deeper. I would share some of my memories with her and she would cry and show me the sympathy I wanted from my mother but never received. Being with her helped me heal a lot. So after a year or so we decided that we both needed our friendship relationship more than we needed an intimate relationship with one another. We both had issues in our lives that we couldn't find the right person to talk to about. And luckily we found one another.

I did sign up to get counseling since it was offered through my health insurance. I went to about 3 or 4 visits to try and talk to someone to help me deal with this. I thought that if I talked to someone that all this pain would somehow go away. So one day this counselor that I had been seeing said to me "do you think by the way that you dressed that maybe you entice your uncle". Now I have a pretty nice looking body and when I was 40 pounds smaller I did look good. I was at her office with a short black mini skirt and a black and white shirt and some white stocking and 3 inch black heels. I think I may have been around 27 or 28. Now in my head I was thinking what the fuck I know this skinny little white bitch did not say what I think she said. That was the last thing I remember her saying to myself. I must have had a black out with anger because I fucked that office up. Then I walked out of her office and went to the front desk and made another appointment to see her the following week. I received a letter in the mail telling me not to come back and that I had to pay for damages I did to her office. I felt so much rage when she said those things to me that it scared me to even discuss what had happened to me let alone how I felt because I didn't know what I would do if they said something stupid like her ass did. I was like dam does everyone think like my momma when it comes to this issue. How is it the victim fault? It's like when a woman gets raped the first thing they do is look at how she was dressed. And some people say "she asked for it look at how she was dressed". Looking a certain way does not give another person the right to violate you.

My relationship with my mom isn't any better. She does things with children and for my children as a grandparent. She will never help me directly. She buys things for my kids like clothes, toys and shoes. She even goes grocery shopping and buys them certain snack and cakes that they like. But as far as me if I were to go near her she wouldn't hug me or touch me if her life depended on it. And god forbid she say she loves me she would rather swallow acid first. As long as I keep my independence she can't bitch about anything that I do in my household.

My dad and I are cool we still have the father and daughter relationship even thou he didn't act like the super hero I wanted him to be in my life. It's the way that he treated me after that keeps me from hating him. I didn't get the cold treatment he comforted me as best as he could. By still being a father to me I guess but my mother well she went to the left. I mean totally pulled my wig back and shocked the fuck out of me by her reaction. And we have a void like the black hole between us.

Whenever I try to show her affection she swallows it up like a black hole and her anger towards me get bigger and the void between us gets wider. Why I will never understand.

How would an only child feel when they see their mother's face light up like a Christmas tree every time she talks about her niece? She lights up like a fagit with a bag of fat dicks. "Oh my God she is married, oh my God she has a job or oh my God she just had another baby." Or the Oh my God she goes to church". And the "Oh my God I'm so happy for her, oh my God this and oh my God that". She never showed any excitement with anything that I did since the truth about what her brother did to me came out of the closet. Instead she finds little ways to show her disgust for me. I can buy her gifts I might get a smile or 10 seconds of happiness but no hugs no kisses and definitely not an OH MY GOD. But my cousin can send her a $5.00 hat and she will scream out a hundred "oh my Gods". Buying her gifts to squeeze some kind of affection from her was a waste of my time and my money. No matter what I do she will never go back to loving me like she once did. Tolerating me yes she does that but loving me no. That monster that violated me gets more of her love than me and I'm the victim. He can call and she doesn't think twice about telling him she loves him. I know she was the oldest of ten children and she would tell me stories of how she protected them while they walked to school. How they had to fight off white kids to get to school and how she was always in front ready to beat someone down while they were getting picked on by the white kids. She told me stories of how she would stand in front and make her siblings and younger cousins stand behind her while she stood up to the white children who was trying to keep them from going to school and fight. She always protected her siblings even when they are monsters she loves them no less. And in this situation she will protect her sibling and let her own child suffer. It doesn't matter how much negative insults you say about any of her siblings she will have one million positive insults to throw back at you defending her sibling.

So my wonderful cousin can do nothing wrong. My cousin is happily married. And her wonderful husband has a cousin. His name is Bay. We talked on the phone for a while. A few months I think about 5 months. We are 1000 miles away so this relationship is far from serious. One day we were talking about him coming to visit me since he has vacation time at his job. He claims he is afraid of flying but probably too cheap to buy a ticket. So he decides to catch the grey hound to where I live. That is about a 24 hour trip on the greyhound and about 50 stops along the way when he could have taken a 4 hour flight. He says he will stay for 2 weeks so I have some vacation time and I take off for a week to hang out with him and show him around the city. I go to pick him up from the bus station and there he is tall, dark and average looking. We get back to my house and I introduce him to my boys and my best friend. Me and her have known each other since I was around 8 years old. But she doesn't really know me she only knows what I want her to know. We go over to my parent's house and I introduce him to my parents and they talk about down south. Him and my mother talk about people from down home. She knows some of his relatives and they gossip at the kitchen table. Then we all have dinner together. It was Sunday and my mother has always cooked a big dinner on Sunday even thou the guest list never changed. So during the first 5 days we went to the museum, mall and out to eat a few times. We went to Niagara Falls to see the falls and to go to the casino. It was still winter time almost spring but cold and he wasn't use to the cold weather.

I had a spare bedroom upstairs and there is where he kept his things. We had sex at night when the kids were sleep and we used protection every time. When the boys woke up in the morning I was in my room and he was in the spare bedroom upstairs.

A friend of mine that I work with is having a birthday party on Saturday. I told her we would come the tickets were $5.00 and I brought a ticket for us and my best friend. The bar was in walking distance of my house less than a 10 minute walk so if we got to drunk we could still make it home. My best friend decides to drive to the party so we piled up in her car. We get there and not too many people are there may be a handful so it was a boring party. My co-worker said don't worry more people are coming so we sit back and have a few drinks and enjoy the free food. After about 2 hours we decide to leave and go to another bar that is farther up the street. My best friend drives us to the next bar it's about 15 minutes away and this bar is packed and the music is blasting. So we are drinking and laughing and I even get on the dance floor and dance with him which is something I don't do because I know I am the only black girl in the world who can't dance. I know I got wasted I don't even remember leaving the bar. I woke up the next morning and he was in my bed sleep but I was naked. I woke him up and asked "what the fuck happened did you have sex with me". And he said "yes" then I asked him "did you at least use a condom?" and he said "no we came home you laid down in the bed and you were laying there sleep and I couldn't help myself". I can't remember all that I said to him but within the next 30 minutes his ass was at the train station on his way back home 1 week early. I guess I caused all of that on myself for being too trustworthy with him. I could have gotten over the fact that he had sex with me while I was totally out of it. I couldn't remember if I said it was okay or not but the fact that burned me up is he couldn't take 3 seconds to put on a condom that was sitting right there in his face on the table next to the bed. I know he had to fight to get my clothes off because the outfit I had on was skin tight and the griddle I had on was even tighter than that.

So about 4 weeks go bye and yes I am pregnant. I called him and told him that I was pregnant and his replay which shouldn't have shocked me at all was "I can't help you if you have it. I have my son and my son mother I have to take care of". I just hung up the phone there was nothing more to say. The next day I called the clinic and made an appointment to have an abortion done. He didn't want it and this was one child I didn't want. The way the child was conceived made me hate it even more. I told my best friend what had happened to me and what I was going to do. She was supportive and she watched my boys for me while I went to the clinic alone. I arrived at the clinic and there were all types of women and girls there some showing and some weren't. Some alone like me and some with their boyfriends, girlfriends or some type of support person. I felt no remorse no guilt as I went through the procedure. I took my sonogram the lady asked me if I wanted to look at it and I told her no. I didn't want to see what that bastard made with me. I didn't want the image in my head in case I felt bad later. Then I had to talk to the councilor lady and answer all her questions and once that was over I waited for my name to be called so I could complete the procedure. I remember feeling totally numb through it all not one tear not any feeling of guilt or remorse. I just wanted it out of me as soon as possible. The procedure took less than a minute then I was up and out and laying in the recovery room. As I laid in the recovery room I looked around at all the women and young girls that was there some were crying some was just laying there numb like I was. I think it may have been an hour and I was free to go home. And I drove home as fast and I could and I went into the house and my best friend was there and I just feel apart as soon as I walked into the door of the house. I just started crying and screaming. My best friend just held me in her arms and let me get it all out of my system. Even thou I went through the procedure feeling numb inside it hurt me. But I knew I could not have that baby the way that child was conceived. I know if I had it I would end up hating that child. I never want to make any difference on the way I treat my children but if I would have had that child there is no telling how I would have treated that child. I know I would have hated it. Just for the 4 weeks I carried it I hated it inside of me. All I could do was ask God to forgive me and understand why I made that choice. I don't know if it was the right choice or the wrong choice to make. If the morning after pill would have been available to me back then maybe I wouldn't have felt bad because I wouldn't have went through that procedure. You take a pill the next day you have a menstrual cycle and everything is flushed out. You never know if you were or weren't pregnant.

I never called him anymore I never told him what I did or what I didn't do. There wasn't going to be any communication between us anymore. I told my cousin what happened between me and husband cousin. She was upset and shocked that he would do something like that. She thought he was a decent guy as wonderful as her husband. But you can't trust everyone. I know she felt bad she kept telling me she was sorry about what happened and I told her it was okay it wasn't her fault. My mother asked where "did he go I thought he was staying 2 weeks" I told her he had an emergency and had to go back home so he had to leave early. I didn't even tell her what happened that would just be another thing she would throw up in my face and remind me of till the day I died.

A few years have gone by and I have had a few unsuccessful relationships so I can't remember because some they were just that quick. I am dating a guy a little younger than me maybe about 2 years younger. We don't have anything in common really other than we are both of the same race. He is a young immature man still lives with momma and daddy those are the worst men to date. But he will do for now. I am not looking for anything serious just trying to fill a void longing for some kind of affection on a regular. I know sex isn't love but sometimes those few moments feel good even if it only last a few moments. At least I am not as disgusted as I was before with having sex. This relationship won't fill the void that I have but it fills a few empty spaces up for a few moments.

So I meet a new guy but I never even introduce him to my family other than my sons. Because my kids live with me so they had to be introduced to him. I ended up getting pregnant about a month into the relationship. I told him that I was pregnant and he faked like he was all happy. We laid in bed he was hoping for a boy and I was hoping for a girl. We joked about what the baby would look like and talk about names. Then the next day this mother fucker comes to the house. He rings the door bell and I go to the door to answer it. Now he is outside the door and has his hand up against the door so I can't open the screen door. This fool tells me he "I don't want to see you anymore and if you decide to have the baby that is on you just give the baby my last name if you chose to have it". Now I am going into bi-polar psycho going to fuck up mode right about now. I am tripping because this fool was just playing happy daddy a few hours ago when we were laying in bed picking out baby names. Now he comes to me with this bull shit less than a day after I told him the news. So I am cussing and screaming at him trying to open the door. But he stopped me from opening the door. Then he said the stupidest shit he could have said "If you wasn't pregnant I would fuck you up for all that shit you are talking". I went into straight Bruce Lee mode and kicked the shit out of the door. His ass and the door went flying. He ran his ass away from the door and jumped into a green Pontiac grand AM that he drove over to my house. I had my metal baseball bat in hand and smashed the shit out of that car while he was trying to get his keys together. It got smashed real good windows and doors. When I got through with that car it looked like it had been in a car wreck. I wonder how he explained that to the insurance company.

So now I am hurt and depressed by what this fool just done to me. I told my boys about my pregnancy and no one else in my family knew except for my boys, my best friend and my cousin. I told my boys not to tell their grandparents about me being pregnant right now. I had to tell my employer because of the doctor visits but other than that it was my little secret. One day I go to the abortion clinic I stood outside debating what to do. I already had 3 kids with no father in their lives and looks like number 4 is going to be in the same boat. I must have stayed outside that building for about an hour. I had already told my boys that another child would be joining them soon. They seemed so happy about it. They were asking me all kinds of questions and they were even talking to my stomach every night. How could I explain it to them what I was thinking about doing. Tell them that I didn't want to go through this bullshit again with my mother that was the only reason I was even considering an abortion was because I didn't want to go to battle with her. After a few moments I finally walk away and went back home.

I am hiding my pregnancy from my parent well so far so good. But the father of this child that I am carrying just happens to work at the same hospital that I go to for my prenatal visits. We haven't talked since the day I smashed his car up with my metal baseball bat. I wonder what he told the insurance company about the damages. I am about 4 months along and I see him in the hallway doing janitorial work. I didn't act a fool right away. I just waited until there was no one in the hall but me and him. He wouldn't even look at me coward as nigga but that's okay. I took the rest of my soda and my left over McDonald's meal and threw it all over the floors of the halls that he had just cleaned. I continued to do this every time I went to the hospital for a doctor visit. I would always go around the time he was working. I would walk the hospital around until I seen him and throw food and drinks all over the floor. And cuss him out while he cleaned up the mess. Not once did he make eye contact with me.

My boys are really into the pregnancy. We are going over baby books together and they are watching programs on television about women being pregnant. And I am keeping them update with everything. But inside I am still afraid to face my family with my new pregnancy. I ended up hooking up with an old neighbor of mine from my child hood. We ran into each other and I was already pregnant and told him what had happened and he said cool he will just tell people that the baby is his. He told me how he had been liking me for years but never took time to talk to me when I got older. Either he was with someone or I was with someone. So towards the 2nd half of my pregnancy him and the boys were my support. They were all excited about her arrival but I tried to act happy but inside I knew I wasn't.

My grandmother died on my father side of the family. I really didn't give a dam she never did shit for me. She treated me more like a leper than a grandchild. I have 3 kids my oldest is 11 now and she never seen any of them. It wasn't like she was a loving relative to me she never treated me like a granddaughter she never treated me like I was even human. So if she went to heaven well when I die I want to go to hell. To me there is no way she deserves to go to heaven. They say right before you die your life flash before your eyes so when you go to God you know what you have to answer for. I wonder what she saw.

So we are at the funeral which is fucked up because it was me, my mom, my dad and his brother are all sitting on a bench together looking like outcast. No one came to speak to my dad or my uncle to tell them they were sorry about his mother passing. I saw people going up to my Aunt and her now husband hugging them and saying how sorry they were. But no one came over to my dad or my Uncle to tell them they were sorry for their lost. There were my dad nieces and nephews were there and the other siblings but they didn't say a word to us and we are in a church. I thought you were suppose to leave all the anger outside the church door when you entered it I guess they didn't get the memo.

Black funerals are the most dramatic places to be if you want to find a new actress or actors just go to a black funeral. And the pastors they need there asses kicked talking about her like he knew her. Shit she hadn't been to church in over 20 years. You would think she went every day and was active in every church event and committee the way they talked about her. When I die just cremate me and call it a day no time to be surrounded by bullshit and acting. Well the rest of my father's family was all together and not one of those mother fuckers spoke like I said. They looked and turned their heads it was cool I was there because for one it was a paid off day from my job well a paid 3 days off and two my dad asked me to be there with him. Other than that the bitch could have died and it still would have been a normal day for me no tears shed. Before she died when she was still living with her daughter she fell down the stairs and broke her hip and her daughter had her placed into a nursing facility. My father went to go see his mother a couple of times while she was there. Out of respect for him he asked if my mother and I could go see his mother because he didn't like seeing his mother in a nursing home. We went to see her to please him over the past couple of years. I watched her slowly forget who we were. I watched as Alzheimer's slowly crept into her mind and take control. She went from speaking and eating on her own to finally laying their lifeless and waiting and hoping in her mind that someone had sympathy on her and feed her. My mother said that when you are evil God has a way of punishing you during death. And in my mind I can't help but wonder what she faces when her time come. The grandchild she couldn't stand was there in her last days. Making sure her hair was comb and she was getting fair treatment. I made sure to ask her if she wanted a treat on my next visit when she was able to communicate. It is good to make sure you give people fair treatment you never know who will be holding you hand in the end.

After the funeral we leave and go to my parent's house. Now the other family members decide to have a family dinner after the funeral. My dad was upset about the death of his mother no matter how shitty she was to me and my mother she was still his mother. So they have this little family dinner after the funeral and didn't invite my dad or my uncle. We are at my parent's house talking about the funeral and how dramatic it was all the screams and crying and holding on to the casket while the pallbearers were trying to put it in the hearse. Black folks know how to put on a good show or give you a good laugh. So my other uncle comes by my dad brother I think out of my thirty something years of life I may have seen him a total of 5 times and that number may be too high. He is a truck driver now and lives down south and he use to be pastor but I guess for money reason he had to pick up trucking. Him and his wife travel on the road together they don't have any children. When he needed money for trucking school and had to pay his mortgage my parents gave it up. Whenever they needed money for whatever reason when falling behind on bills I guess they called my parents and got it. Mind you he didn't call his mother or any of his stuck up ass sisters for the money. He called the outcast my father. So my uncle walks in the door I think I said something like "here you come now after yal had your little family dinner didn't think to come get my dad but you know him when you need money sent to you". This fool turns around and tells my dad "Allen you need to tell your daughter to stay in her place". When I heard those words all kinds of shit came out of my mouth. I went off I even made up some new profanity words just for his ass. Then my mom came running in the room telling me to "get the fuck out of her house". I wasn't shocked she was probably dying to say those words to me anyway she just needed a reason. I looked at my dad and walked away and stayed away for about 2 months.

During the two month time that I wasn't speaking to my parents my dad had suffered a mild stroke 2 weeks after the death of his mother. No one bothered to tell me. Not even my mother's favorite niece or her mother. I had been in contact with them both and they knew what had happened but didn't mention it to me.

I go into labor towards the end of March one night. And I called the boys down stairs and told them I was ready to have the baby. I was having contractions about 20 – 30 minutes apart. I was waiting it out until they got closer because I didn't want to have to go back home. Now kids are a trip. My water broke that was the first time I had ever seen that happen out of my previous pregnancies. The boys run and get towels and started boiling water in the microwave and started telling me to lay down on the floor. I asked them "What in the hell are you doing" they told me "it's okay we have already watched the video we know how to deliver the baby". I hurried up and called my girlfriend who was also about 6 months pregnant to come take me to the hospital. That was funniest thing I have ever heard of. I give them all the love in the world because they were ready to be mid wives but not on my shift as long as they have a hospital less than 5 minutes away I will not be delivering at home.

We make it to the hospital around 4:30 a.m and at 7:03 a.m. comes the smallest little girl in the world 6 pounds 8 ounces. She was the cutest baby girl in the history of baby girls. She had a head full of black curly hair and came in the world wanting all the attention she could get. I was in the hospital for 5 days and every day she had to stay in the room with me. Whenever they would put her in the nursery she would scream because she wanted someone to be talking to her all the time. I think that is because her 3 brothers talked her to death when I was carrying her.

I am on my way home from the hospital my girlfriend she comes and pick me up and take me home. Now my mother and my adopted sister show up 10 minutes after I get home wanting to see the new baby. My girl friend told them the night she took to the hospital and my mother went by the house to get my boys until I came home from the hospital. My mother had just forgotten that she told me to get the fuck out of her house 2 months ago. I am too tired to argue with her I just wanted to enjoy my new baby girl. She asks me if she could take her over to see my dad because he was too sick to come over but wanted to see her. Now when she says sick I think of a cold or something like that she never mentioned that he had a stroke 2 months ago. I tell her fine I have to run out and get some formula and other things that I did not get for the baby.

I arrived at my parent's house about 2 hours later. They only lived 5 minutes away from me. I go inside my parent's house and the first thing a see is my dad in his chair. I could have screamed. I knew by looking at him that something was wrong. Instead I looked at my sister and my mother and ask them what the fuck happened. They explained to me that they did not want to tell me about it because my girl friend had told them I was pregnant and they did not want to upset me while I was pregnant. I accepted the answer but I was still mad. He was my father and regardless of the situation someone should have told me something. He was in the hospital for 3 weeks after his stroke. He was still able to walk but needed help with a cane or he needed someone to lean on. His speech was slurred and his face was droopy on one side and his ankles were swollen a lot for some reason. He was so happy to see me and I was just as happy to see him. He loved his new grandchild a little tiny girl. She looked exactly like I did in my newborn pictures. You couldn't tell if it was a picture of me or of her. Within a few days she had more clothes than a department store. My mother ran out and brought her all type of clothes. I accepted them but I knew in my mind she will have something smart to say to me about it. But I didn't care what she had to say my daughter made my dad so happy when she was around him. And that is all that I wanted for him during this time was happiness.

I didn't hear any bullshit remarks from my mother. Which was very surprising to me I was just waiting and staying on guard at all times. Her, my dad and my sister were too busy spoiling the new baby. She mainly stayed with them Monday

–Friday and with me Friday night –Sunday. For some reason my father wanted to her around him all the time.

I had signed up for college again for the third time. I was working a new job and in order for me to move up the corporate ladder I had to go back to school and get another degree. I had already been to college twice so far. And I have received two associate degrees but now I was going for my bachelors. My mom is starting to complain about me going to school again so she would say "aren't you done with school". That is the problem with black folks. When one of us is trying to do better where does the support go? Well I shouldn't be shocked because I never received any supporting advice or words from her why should she start now.

Well all good things come to an end. My uncle my mother's brother comes to town for a visit. He has now re-married and I guess brought his new wife to see his family up North. He brings my Big Momma and his new wife and her children. This caught me totally off guard no one mentioned it to me. I go over to drop my daughter off to my mother's house. I have a part time job at a nursing home that I work on the weekends for 4 hours during the morning. I see a strange van in my parent's driveway. And my parent's vehicles are parked on the street which is very strange. And I see that the van in the drive way with some Florida plates on it. I get out of my van wondering who is here we don't have any family in Florida. I walk up on the porch I see my mother, my Big Momma and the monster all sitting there talking. My mother wouldn't even look me in my face. I walked over to my Big Momma and gave her a big hug. Turned around walked into the house and looked at my father and I told him "This is some fucked up shit". I grab everything that I seen that belonged to my daughter and threw it in a bag. That monster wouldn't even look my way he kept his head turned the other way. I can't put into words how much anger I felt towards my parent's. I had not seen him in 20 years and here he is living it up like he did nothing wrong. Had my Big Momma not been there I know things would have been a lot different. I know my reaction would have definitely been different. I know I didn't want to hurt her and act a fool. She has never seen that side of me and I didn't want to show it to her. So it took everything inside of me to not snap. So in a turn of events I put my daughter into daycare when she was around 4 months old and tell my parents that she isn't coming over there anymore. Well my mother's dear old brother and his new family hang around for about a month. I did follow him one day while they were out driving around the city. I thought about killing him. I thought about having him jumped in public. But I did none of that. So after he left and went back to Florida it would be another 3 months before I would speak or see my parents again.

My dad called one day and said he missed seeing his little granddaughter. His health hasn't been the greatest and he said he just loves being around her and he tells me how happy he is when she is around him. So out of respect for my dad I grant his wishes. My mother must tolerate me because my father wants to see his granddaughter. And he hasn't seen his grandsons in a while also. And if we're not speaking he can't see neither of them. So we go back to the old schedule that we had when she was first born. She is over their house Monday – Friday and I get her on the weekends.

Almost 18 months go by and my father is starting to get sick. He is back and forth to the doctors and they say it's from the stroke he had. Then one day he goes and the doctor and they tell him he has stomach cancer. It was a Friday I remember the day because it was my birthday. I took that day off and decided to hang out with him at the doctor office. They said he had stomach cancer and it was in his colon and liver and kidneys as well. They said that maybe if he received some chemo therapy that it would either slow the cancer growth or shrink some of the cancer growth. My mother was willing to try anything if it would make him live another day. I decided to take unpaid medical leave for 4 months to be by his side while he received his chemo-therapy. We went to his first session of chemo-therapy that Monday. It took a lot out of him. He couldn't walk he was so weak but he still kept smiling. My daughter is there and he tells me to place her on his lap. Even thou he is weak he stills try to play with her. He was too weak to walk upstairs so we had to buy a couch bed. And put it down stairs for him to lay on and sleep on. We went to chemo-therapy for the second session then one day he refused to eat. I could always get him to listen to me when it came to taking medicines and going to doctor visits. My mom called me over and said “your dad isn’t eating for me can you please come over and get him to eat for me he hasn’t ate all day.” I rushed over there as fast as I could. And I talked to him about how I needed him to eat and drink and I didn’t want him to leave me and could he please just try to eat for me. He did he took a few spoonful of food then he said he was “tired and ready to go”. I am like go where. He was ready to die. He was tired of struggling to live and was ready to be at peace. He was in perfect health just 4 week earlier before he knew he had cancer. He was walking around and laughing. He had handed me his Christmas list and telling me what he wanted for Christmas like always. But as soon as he found out he had cancer again and agreed to this chemo-therapy it just killed him instantly one session took the life right out of him. I think the doctor knew there was no hope for him but they wanted that money. I think without the chemo-therapy he would have lasted a little longer. I guess that is selfish of me to want to hold on to my dad even if it met he had to suffer.

It was Christmas Eve my mother finally called 911 to come get him and take him to the hospital. I couldn’t say anything all I could do was look and try to be as strong as I could be. I remember I grabbed his gifts for from under the tree and I told him “we can open your gifts tonight so you can see what the kids picked out for you”. We drove to the hospital and when we got there the doctor told us that the cancer had spread to his brain and the only thing they could do was put him in a coma so he wouldn't be in pain until he passes. We went to his room before they put him into a coma. He asked me "what are you taking up this time you always got your ass in school". I told him "I am trying to get a bachelor degree in accounting so I can make more money." The nurse was putting the medicine in his IV the last words he said to me was "I am so proud of you" then he went into a coma. We stayed in the hospital room for 9 days. I wouldn't leave I brought all my school books up there and was working on papers for school. I don't even think I changed my clothes. I didn't want to leave him not for a second. I guess I kept thinking that he was going to jump up and be okay. I knew he could hear me so I talked to him. I turned the television on so we could watch our favorite TV shows and had a conversation with him like he was answering me back. Maybe my mind was assuming what he would say to me if he could answer me back. But no one was talking but me yeah I know completely thrown off. Then I think the next day his 2 sisters and his niece show up at the hospital. I don't know how they knew he was there. I didn't tell them maybe when my mother told his brother and he told them I really don't know. But it tripped me out when they came into the room. His one sister has never been to my parent's house to visit and she lived less than 5 minutes away. His other sister and her daughter we haven't seen them in over 22 years. But when he is dying and can no longer speak or open his eyes to see them here they come like a loving family. The same one's that was at their mother's funeral 2 years earlier and wouldn't speak to him are not shedding tears at his death bed. But here you come when he is dying and can't talk to you. How ignorant. They walked into the room my mother acted like they were invisible and I don't blame her. Then his oldest sister goes over to his bed and start rubbing his hand like she actually cared for him. When she was done she turned to me and said "well I guess this will be the last time I see you" and they left the room. I knew my father could still hear and I wanted to go off but I wanted his parting to be peaceful so I kept my cool. I wouldn't see them or have contact with them anymore anyway so cussing them out would be a waste of energy even if it would have felt good. It was 7:15 a.m New Year's eve and I am in the hospice room with my dad and I was talking to him about the news and the weather telling him about all the snow that was falling outside. I had finally let the kids come and stay the night in the hospice room because a New Year was coming and we were celebrating it with grand dad. I had just assumed that he will bring in the New Year with us. I was talking to him and he was still breathing I walked away for a minute to get a glass of juice. The nurses came in and they were giving him his morning bath. When they were done I walked back over to his bed and he wasn't breathing and I started screaming as loud as I could "Daddy". My mother started running over to the bed and I remember my mother shaking me and telling me "to be quiet and just let him go in peace he isn't suffering anymore" and stop screaming. I didn't want to let him go that was only part of love that I had from a parent and I was trying to hold on to it for as long as I could. When he died I knew right then I was solo.

We didn't have a funeral for him or a memorial. His wishes were to be cremated and buried down in Mississippi were my Granny is buried at. He had always loved my mother's side of the family and they had always loved him. We didn't have any of his family come over to the house if they weren't celebrating his life don't come celebrate his death. It was just me, my kids, my mother, my adopted sister and my boyfriend at the time and one my foster sister one of the little orphans who had been living with me for a while now. The other orphan was locked up in jail for drug charges I think at the time he died. I got drunk that day. We acted silly the whole night doing karaoke songs and talking about all the funny stuff my father use to do. Talking about the ass whipping we got from him and all the "wild game" he us to cook for us. What city girl you know grew up eating rabbit, squirrel and turtle soup? To other people that was country but to my family especially my daddy that was normal food.

My dad and I had certain movies we would watch together on the holidays "The greatest story ever told" and the "Ten commandments" I haven't been able to watch those movies since his death. I tired but I can't make it through the movies before falling apart. All the T.V shows that we use to watch together I don't watch anymore. I miss him every day of my life. It's not a moment that goes by that I don't wish he was still here with me. I still celebrate his birthday. I still buy him a cake. A part of me won't let him go.

I still had about 1 semester left of school at the time of my dad's death. I did so bad afterwards I got either a C or a D for that semester in two of my classes. I didn't care as long as didn't have to repeat a class it didn't matter to me about my grade point average. I remember my Economic teacher telling " I was the worse student she had ever had" and that she hoped I never sign up to take another one of her classes. She even did one on one session with me that semester to help me pass but I was so distraught about my dad that I don't remember a dam thing she said to me.

After releasing some of the pain that was inside of me to my man I came to a pause no words spoken between us. That night I just laid there and thought about all the funny memories I had of my father.

Here I am with this wonderful man and a part of me wants to hurt him. His touch is starting to make me mad. I have tried over and over to start fights with both physical and verbal. But he refuses to fall into that scenario with me. Instead he just ignores me. I should be happy that I have such a caring person in my life but instead that person my uncle created wants nothing more but to cause pain on anyone who is showing me love in my life. It is hard to explain why I want to hurt him so much. I know in my heart that he will never hurt me. So I continue my story to a person who is willing to listen. And then I snap!

Part 4

Fallen on deaf ears

Reality has just sat in and it is eating my flesh down to the bone
Here I am surrounded by millions to see but I am in this world alone
My screams are echoing through the air in despair hoping all is not gone

Do you hear me? Have my efforts fallen on deaf ears?

Pains sit in and play upon my weak body and shatter every bone
All eyes on me but why are they blind and leave me in this world alone
My screams are getting louder for everyone to hear but I fear their souls
Are gone

Do you hear me? Have my efforts fallen on deaf ears?

No more strength left in me my body is drained to the bone
People stop and stare but they don't see that I am beaten, tired and
Alone my screams are getting weaker not another sound to make my hope is
Gone

All my efforts have been in vain for they have fallen on deaf ears

I have always had violent tendencies towards men in a majority of my relationships. Some of my ex-boyfriends would definitely agree that I am thrown the fuck off. I was called bipolar a million times before I even knew what bipolar was. I can treat them like kings and turn around and try to kill them in a matter of seconds. I would take the smallest issue and blow it up just so I could yell and scream at them. Or even get a chance to be physical with them. I guess it was a way of blowing off steam or releasing whatever I felt inside that I could not explain. I had and still do have a lot of anger built up inside of me. It was a man who caused this anger so men are my primary target when it comes to releasing some of it.

My earliest memory of snapping on my children which were boys was around the time I became pregnant with my daughter. My kids did something I can't really remember what they did. But all 3 of them were in trouble they always lied to protect one another. And I kept on telling them to just be honest regardless of what is done. I can't help you if you are not honest with me. But if I have your back just to find out your lying I am going to kick your ass. I love my boys to death. They love me when I don't even love myself. I over compensated because their fathers were not and still aren't in their lives. So they are a little spoiled at times. Then there are times when I have to put my foot down and keep them in check. Well one day they were in trouble for something and I know I was mad because they kept lying to me to protect one another. I remember I told them to strip down to their underwear because I was about to tear their asses up for lying to me. I had all 3 of them in the bedroom. I started swinging my leather belt at them. They were running around the room and crying. And then somehow I must have blacked out. I remember feeling so much anger towards them but it should not have been that much to the point where I was trying to kill them. I wanted to hurt them badly because they were boys. Not for what they did but because of the sex that they were. Hearing them scream gave me more energy to keep hitting them. Somehow I went from using the belt to using my fist. I was punching them repeatedly. I remember my oldest son who was around 11 at time laying on top of his 2 brothers who were 6 & 5 at the time I think. He was willing to take all the punishment for them like I had done for my uncle years ago. I stopped and looked at my son he had so many bruises on his body and I had gave him a black eye. I just started screaming and yelling. I grabbed them and told them how sorry I was and that I would never hit them again. I had turned into a monster towards the ones I loved my boys. I couldn't explain to them what was wrong with me. I sat and thought about all the other times I had hit them out of anger that had nothing to do with them or what they had done. They did not deserve the punishment I had given them. I just had to sit and play back in my head what I had done to them and during the initial punishment they were suppose to receive I started thinking about my uncle and snapped on my own kids. I must have told them I was sorry a thousand times. I told my son I didn't mean to give him a black eye he lied and told people at school he was fighting with his brother and got hit in the eye. I knew then that is was not safe for me to discipline my children. I had to resort to taking away toys, games, not letting them go outside. I had to find different forms of punishment that was safer for me and them. I never want to hurt my boys like that again.

The hardest thing for me is having to function in this world without concentrating on what was done to me. Keeping up a smile and acting as normal as possible when every moment you feel like giving up inside but still you are smiling to everyone. Trying to look in the mirror everyday and find that person that everyone else sees. Where is that beautiful woman I hear so much about? I look in the mirror and I don't see her. Every day is a challenge for me. I could have ran to drugs for relief but I didn't. I never had an experience that caused me to mess with drugs other than alcohol. I had it at my disposable but never engaged in it. I think maybe God was keeping me strong in that area even thou I felt weak as hell.

I still continued to go to church every Sunday like I have been doing all my life. Me, my mother, my sister and my children. All went to church together like one big happy family in the eyes of society. We went to a Baptist church that was in the community. A new younger pastor had taken over the church. He was handsome and single. He was a newly divorced man and had just brought a house in the community. Women from all around the neighborhood started joining the church. Everybody wanted to be in control of some organization to try and impress the new pastor. Women became ushers and choir members out of the blue. We didn't even have a choir before we all sang together when it was time to sing. Now we had a senior choir and a young adult choir. They even started an Usher Board and women's committee all within a matter of three months. And I had been going to the church for 5 years. The same women that were now members had been sitting on their porches or walking by for the past five years and never stepped foot inside of the church. But now they are members and organizing committees.

The church was always full on Sunday with women when the new young pastor took over. I had been a member of this church for over 5 years and was lucky to see 10 members on a good Sunday. But this pastor had this thing were you would go around the church and hug your neighbor. I was not a big fan on hugging. I would rather shake a members hand and walk away. But he always push the issue for members to hug him especially women. He would ask me for a hug and I would refuse. Or I would give him a half ass hug and walk away quickly. I even told him once to shake my hand or keep it moving. My mother even felt uncomfortable about hugging him she even mentioned it to my dad one day about the way he hugs and that she didn't like it and he told her either "stop hugging him or me and my 38 are coming up there for church service". I thought I was the only one who felt uncomfortable about his hugs but I also spoke with 2 other female members and they said the same thing like his hug are too long or he pulls you to close to his body when he does it. We even suggested to some of the members that we should walk around and speak to one another for a few moments like we did before he took over the church. But the female majority sided with new pastor. Since he didn't see anything wrong with hugging the other single hungry women didn't either.

One day I was in the basement of the church. I was about 4 months pregnant with my daughter and was going to the bathroom. You couldn't tell that I was pregnant at the time with my daughter I still wore the same clothes whenever my stomach showed a little I would just un-tuck the shirt. So anyway I was in the basement and he was down there doing what I don't know. He says to me 'you are so mean to me come over here and give your pastor a good hug". I told him "no" and continued walking to the bathroom. So this fool grabs me and pushes me against the wall and started to grind on me. I snapped and ended up cussing out the pastor in the basement of the church. The members were running down there to see what was wrong. I walked back up stairs still screaming then I walked outside the church. I was screaming he was a nasty mother fucker and that he wasn't shit. My mom was mad as hell at me. I had embarrassed her in front of the church folk. I walked home and I guess service continued without me. I got home told my boyfriend at the time what happened he was pist off and wanted to go fuck up the pastor. I told him to calm down and I told him to forget it I just won't go there anymore. I called my dad and told him what happened. He understood my actions and he was like "yeah your mother said he was little to fresh with his hugs". I told him I didn't like it and I went off. So when service was over my mother came to my house to drop off the kids from church. I was trying to tell her what happened and she just said she didn't want t o hear it and why did I have to act that way. She didn't even give me a chance to explain why I did what I did. So I just said fuck it and I won't be attending that church anymore. So from that day on she and my sister went to church no little happy family portrait for society. Sorry to say 6 months later the young healthy pastor died in the doctor office while getting a stress test. He was sitting in the waiting room after taking his test and had a massive heart attack and died. A new pastor took over the church but I never attended on a regular basis. I went only for night watch service or Easter. Other than that I would watch church programs on television or read it on the internet.

But I also snapped again when I had my daughter. She had to be a few weeks old I was still on maternity leave. I was sleep and I remember that I fell asleep with her next to me in the bed. I woke up and she was gone. I went and walked up to the front of the house and I seen my boyfriend at the time with my daughter. She was naked and he was standing over laughing and talking silly to her. It was completely innocent but in my mind all I saw was my naked daughter and a man standing over her. I snapped I went crazy on my boyfriend. I started screaming and hitting him and telling him to leave my daughter alone. He grabbed me and started shaking me asking me "what the fuck is wrong with you, you were sleep the baby woke up I picked her up and changed her diaper because she had shit all over her and her clothes so I washed her up and was putting some fresh clothes on her". I started crying that was all I could do and I just walked away and went back to my bedroom. He gave me a few moments to calm down before he came back there.

Later on that night he asked me what the hell was wrong with me and why did I go off on him like that. I had never told him about my uncle. I didn't go into details. I just told him that my uncle use to molest me when I was younger. He knew my uncle because we were neighbors growing up and they were classmates in high school. He was shocked because he knew him and was tripping because they were also friends. Then he said that explains why you never what to be naked around me or in bed. Why sexually you don't participate in oral sex a lot and you're always trying to cover up. And why I have a hot and cold switch with him. One moment I can't breathe without him and the next I can care less if he lives or dies. We never talked about my uncle again. He never asked for details and I never gave him any. But he made sure that if he played with my daughter or changed her diaper that I was around and everything was okay. He spent a lot of time with my boys and helping me with my daughter but I could always tell he was paranoid when he with her because he was scared I was going to snap again.

I ended the conversation by asking my future husband if he still wanted to be with me. I have shared so much with him. And he has tolerated so much. I did notice that after I started sharing my life with him he made dam sure my ass was sleep before he closed his eyes. I am so grateful that I have this man in my life that is willing to help me deal with all of these crazy emotions that I have. And feelings inside that I can't express in words. There are nights where I just lay there and cry and don't even know why I am crying. But he just holds me tight in his arms and let me cry. Crying is good for the soul so why should I hold back the tears.

Part 5

Time to heal

Wounded

My tears flow from my eyes but your hands reach out and catch them so I
Am not left
Wounded
I am surrounded by so many puddles but you quickly kneel down and soak
Them up
Open wounds cover my body that no one had tried to stitch but you stay so I
Am not left
Wounded
My back is nearly broken and I cannot stand and my legs can barely walk

But you come and give me leverage like an invisible cane

So I Am not left

Wounded

How many times have I gotten drunk in my lifetime? How many times have I gotten drunk and not remember what the hell I did the night before? How many times have I gotten drunk and woke up with someone that I couldn't even remember how the fuck we met? Too many times for me to count or try to remember. Drinking has always been a way for me to escape my personal misery. But no matter how much I drank I always made it back home in one piece. I would drink and sometimes I would go to my parent's house. I was just hurting inside and I wanted them acknowledge that pain. I would just pass out on their porch and be pissy ass drunk. Sometimes when I would go to my house I would just lay in my front yard and cry and scream that no one loved me. My neighbors didn't like it but they never tried to help me. They didn't know what was going on all they knew was that their crazy neighbor was drunk again and outside acting a fool. It didn't matter if it was raining or snowing. I would either make it to my front yard or my parent's porch and there I cried until I would pass out and go to sleep. Sometimes they would let me crawl me up on in the doorway of the living room and sleep at door if I wasn't too pissy drunk. Or sometimes they would just leave me on the porch and whenever I woke up I would just go back home. My kids were too young and they didn't know or understand why I was crying so much. They would sometimes sit with me and tell me they loved me. My oldest son would take the car keys and my purse so I couldn't leave and go back out. We make jokes about it now. There was one time I sat in the grass in the front yard while it was raining outside and I started singing old Whitney Houston songs with a big jug of Rossi wine. And another time when I was drunk and they took my car keys and locked me out of the house and watched me from a front window cussing about how no one loved me until I fell asleep in the grass on the front lawn. And they pulled me inside the hallway were I finished sleeping off my liquor. There was another time when I got drunk and started calling people in my past that hurt me and cussing them out on the phone. They are all jokes to my kids now that we sit around and talk about the past events but to me it was something else.

We sit and laugh about the time one of my little orphan sister's came and picked up the boys to take them out to get ice cream. She pulls up in a new Pontiac Grand AM. I asked her where the car came from and she says that one of her friends let her borrow it for a while. Now she never had a driver license in her life she always had a permit but would never go and take the driving test to get her license. The boys were all excited about driving around with her in this new fancy car. While they were out driving around with her and some guy's spotted her driving in their neighborhood. They pulled up and started chasing her in the car with my boys inside of it. When she came back to the house the car was riddled with bullet holes. Thank God no one got hurt or killed. She forgot to tell me the car was stolen and that she had robbed the guys that were chasing her of some money, drugs and that car. The things we do to keep a dollar in our pocket. Even through all this craziness there are still things that happened in my life that I can look back and laugh more about than cry. My boys still talk about being chased in the car and being shot at and her screaming at them to get down on the floor of the car. They wonder like me how did I go through all of this and make it out alive.

The hardest thing for me is to trying to get my uncle out of my head. No matter how drunk or how happy I am those negative thoughts and feeling sometimes crawl back into my life. When I get like that I do get depressed and yes I do have suicidal thoughts but I try to focus on my kids and draw off of their love for me. And I try to keep from putting myself and them through that experience again. There were times were I would get so depressed and no one around me could figure out what the hell was wrong with me because everything seemed so happy in my life. I would either eat up everything in sight or go days without eating. Or I would sleep for long hours at a time or go days without sleep. For the men that had to deal with me I know that during the time they lived with me it was pure hell. Mainly because they didn't know about my past that was something that I didn't always share. I was scared that I was going to get the same cold treatment my parents had given me when they found out about it.

I have believed in God since I could remember. I was taught to believe in him and pray to him. My father never attended church. The only time I seen him go to a church was when my great grandmother past and when his own mother past away. He wasn't that good at reading but he knew the Bible and he knew all the stories in them. Even thou he had his moments when he would act a fool he still found God before he died. He spent his youthful years raising pure hell in the world and when he had gotten too old to raise hell he started looking for God. He would talk to me about believing in God when he got older. And that God could deliver me from all things. And if I believed in God I would be blessed, healed, I would be loved beyond belief. If I had God in my life I could do all the things I wanted to do. I just had to believe and pray to him. I prayed for God to heal me. I prayed for God to protect me. I prayed for God to just let me know he is there and listening to me and working on a solution. I can't count how many times I cried out to God asking him to help me or somehow just erase these memories from my mind. Just waking up in the middle of night and crying until I had no more tears left in my eyes to cry. They say if you pray and ask God for help he will answer. Well in my mind it was like the memories were still here and the pain is still here. Why is God letting me suffer with this pain? What did I do that was so wrong that I deserved to hurt like this? I remember getting mad at God sometimes because he let this happen to me. God controlled everything under the sun so he was in control of my uncle's actions. Sometimes I blamed him more than my uncle. My uncle was the devil and God was supposed to protect me from him. I was a constant church member at our church. I participated in church events and programs and helped who ever asked for my help and sometimes before they could ask I was already helping them. So why did God let me get tortured by my uncle and then again by my mother emotionally. Then one day I realized that out of every negative situation that happens in your life you have to always find the positive and make sure that the positive out shines the negative. Sometimes it can shine so bright that it looks like there is no negative situation there. So whenever people looked at me I made sure the positive shone brighter than the negative. I could be dead ass broke but was still smiling like I had a million dollars in my pocket. My gas could be cut off and I was still smiling like I was going home to cook a big dinner. My mortgage could be behind but I will smile still. I may not know how the hell I was going to feed my kids the next day but I kept smiling. No matter how much I use to close my eyes and see my uncles face and relive some of the memories I made sure those around me seen me smiling. No one ever saw my negative image because I drowned it out with positive. My life had been surrounded by negative events and it was time for me to let the positive events shine through.

Waking up in the morning in its self is a positive event.

It is said that when God wants you to do something or when he is trying to change you, he will have to strip you of everything that is negative in order for you to walk the path he has made for you. Not the path we want or the one we think we should have. But the one he has already cut out for you. His path is a positive path and you cannot carry that luggage that you purchased along the way while traveling your own path can't come with you on his path. Everything in your life happens to you for a reason. It is either a learning experience or is used to strengthen you or both. And it could even be to help or strengthen someone around you.

I had been with my boyfriend for almost 4 years. I had grown so close to him that I could predict what he was about to say. Now this is the same guy that I started dating when I was pregnant with my daughter. The day after I had my daughter he comes to the hospital with an engagement ring. But when you think you know someone that well you can always sense when something isn't right. I knew someone else was in the picture. I didn't have proof but his actions towards me changed when we were about two years into the relationship. And one sign is when they stop making love to you in that special way and giving you that attention that you are use to getting. You know when your dick has been somewhere else. I don't care how much they wash it. If you know your dick real good you know when it's hitting something else and the same for men. I blocked it out of my mind because I only had 2 semesters left and 5 classes left and I would have my bachelor degree. And plus my dad had just lost his fight with cancer at this time. And I needed that degree to help take care of my children because I know firsthand a nigga won't help you with shit. The best back to have is your own. So my devilish mind came up with a plan. Whenever I thought he was going to hang out late I would sneak laxatives into his food and take all the toilet tissue out of the house and leave. Sometimes he would run back home complaining about his stomach was upset. I would laugh to myself "mother fucker won't be fucking her tonight". I even took some heart medicine and blood pressure medicine that use to belong to my father and put it in his food. He was light headed and dizzy he didn't know what the hell was happening to him. And sometimes I would put sleeping pills in his food and he would sleep for 10 to 12 hours. He would go to sleep Friday night and wake up Sunday morning. He didn't know what was wrong with him. He went to about a million doctor appointments and they he was telling them of all the strange things that had been happening to him. They check him for colon cancer because of the diarrhea. Put him on blood pressure medicine because of the dizziness. Start treating him for sleep apnea because of the long hours he would sleep they even gave him a breathing machine. All the while I was there holding his hand comforting him like I always did. I never changed my behavior towards him. Never showed a sign of what I was doing. Me spiking his food went on for almost two years probably would have killed him sooner or later had he not left me.

I was having problems with my menstrual cycle for about 5 or 6 years. My cycle would be so heavy and so long I wanted to die. Then one day I went to the doctor's office and she told me I had fibroid tumors in my uterus and I needed a hysterectomy. That was the only option I had unless I wanted to wait and have more children. I told her she was crazy I have 4 children if I get lonely I will buy a dog. So I told my boyfriend what was needed and told him that my surgery was scheduled in 2 weeks. The night before my surgery he got up and left and told me he was going out for minute. I told him "you know I am having my surgery in the morning I need to be at the hospital by 6 a.m." he replied "I know I will be back home around 4". I went to sleep woke up and he was not there. I called his cell phone and he would not answer so as a last resort I had to call my mother and ask her to drop me off at the hospital because she was going to help watch the kids for me while I was in the hospital. While I was at the hospital he never showed up or called. I had my surgery and when I came out of recovery my mother was there. I asked her had she heard from him and she said no. I received a morphine shot and was out cold until the next day. I woke up the next day called him a few times and the phone was cut off. I was tripping because I had paid the phone bill a day before my surgery why is this number not in service. My mother came to see me on the third day. I asked her had she heard from him and she said no. I was worried and nervous I thought something had happened to him. I knew he was in the streets and things were getting hot. I thought maybe he had gotten into it with someone and was killed or had gotten shot. My mind was running with all kinds of scernios. It's the fifth day and my mother comes to pick me up late in the afternoon because she had to pick the kids up from school first. I arrived home and my oldest son agrees to stay the night with me. It's kind of dark in the house and I was too weak to go past the front door. So I took my pain pills and laid on the couch by the front door for the rest of the night.

The next day I woke up early in the morning. I looked around the house and noticed that there were some items missing. These items belonged to my boyfriend. I walk to the bedroom and every item in there that was his was gone. I went to the kitchen he had emptied out the cabinets and the freezer and the deep freezer in the basement. Not only did he take all his belonging but he took the food also. I was mad as hell I called my mother and told her what had happened. I was hurt beyond belief this was a man who I had been with for 4 years straight shared everything with him. My boys were calling him daddy. I was fucked up in my head for a minute. I was trying to recover from my surgery, finish my last class for school and my final exam was in 2 weeks. I was still dealing with the death of my father who had just past 3 months prior. I don't even smoke but I started smoking cigarettes that day like I had been a smoker all my life. I went to his mother house who was nothing but a veteran crack head she told me she knew all along what he was planning she had told him. She said she couldn't betray him and tell me because she loved her son. Well her son only wanted her monthly SSI check and she only wanted the crack he was selling. He need some extra money from her and had to explain what his plans were in exchange for free crack she kept her mouth shut. She even told me who the woman was and that she had met her a few times. Come and find out the woman he left me for was a co-worker of mine. A white woman the things a black man will do to have a white woman on his arm. The two of them moved to Atlanta while I was in the hospital having surgery. But when you think you have something better than what you already have you better think twice and hard! So after he left me and moved with her and they got settled into their new home she ended up putting him out and having another man move in with her. I always told him "that hussle isn't going to last forever make sure you have some kind trade skills as a backup". But he wouldn't listen. He got down in the ATL and couldn't get his hussle on and she put his black ass out and back to Buffalo he came. But he couldn't come back to me when I seen him he couldn't even look me in the eyes. He just held his head down and walked away.

Well I was out of work for 4 months after my surgery recovering. I received my degree but wasn't able to attend my graduation because of the surgery but that's okay I had my piece of paper. Now when you have God helping you change and helping you to heal like I said he strips you of everything that mean no good to you. I was mourning my boyfriend hard as hell but God wasn't through stripping me just yet. I had just returned back to work after being off for 4 months when one night my house caught on fire while we were sleep. It was about 4 in the morning and an electrical fire started upstairs in the walls of my son room. And before we knew it there were flames everywhere. We all made it out unharmed but my house was gone that I had worked so hard to keep. I went through the insurance company and that took about 4 months to complete the paperwork. My mother let us stay with her while I handled everything with the house. How I wished that I stayed at a hotel. That woman made me miserable complaining about us being there. She told me that we could stay there that is didn't make sense to stay in a hotel room that was a waste of money. But listening to her complain about us being there and how she will be so glad when we get out of her house made me want to just go stay at the homeless shelter. I even gave her half of the check I received from the insurance company $10,000 and still she complained.

My house fire was on the news and the next day my son father whom I had a restraining order against came with his mother and grandmother asking did he need anything. I was shocked because I just spent the last 8 years living a block away from you and your family and not once did they come see him. I just simple told them if you want to buy him something then go ahead. Of course they came back with an outfit and some socks and underwear and never came back again.

They did rebuild my home but when it came time for the final inspection the city failed it. Said something about the upstairs bathroom toilet was too close to the wall. At first I was upset and mad because the contractor said if I wanted it fix I would have to pay for it out of my pocket. And my final decision came to sell the house and let the new home owner deal with the code violation. So now my man is gone and my house the only thing left is my job. I have been with this company for about 4 years. I never had a problem with anyone or a complaint. I always learned as much as I could while employed there. I went back to college just so I could move up in this company. I was starting in my new position and now I have a new supervisor. I didn't like her and she never have liked me and many people in the company didn't like her. She always had and probably still do have a snotty attitude. She talked down to everyone but no one could say thing because she was the top boss buddy. I knew she didn't want me there because one of her comments to me was "you didn't do well in your interview but Kathy wanted to give you a chance and I didn't". She made sure every day that I had working under her was hell. I complained to Kathy about her comments and how she treated me and of course she took her side because they were friends in work and outside of work. My manger she told me that it was "my attitude" and that I "don't address her authority when she speaks to you" what I am suppose to say hail Hitler. It got to the point where I was about to fuck this pregnant snotty bitch up. I was the only black person on that team and even my white co-workers seen how she treated me and seen that she was giving me strife on purpose. So one day I was at my breaking point. I had come in to work early to run some reports for the end of the month no one was in the department but me. I remember sitting there and talking out loud to God. I was crying because my job had become so stressful and I wanted to quit but I couldn't because that was the only income I had. And I was the sole support my children had. I had been staying with my mother for the past 4 months since my house burned down and that was not going so good. And I just sat there and said "god if it is meant for me to stay in this job I will just give me the strength to deal with it if it is not meant for me to be here give me the strength to get up and leave and never look back".

When you go and ask God to help you be very careful because you may not be expecting the answer that you want. He gave me the strength I asked for. His voice is unexplainable but I heard it loud and clear. He told me what city to move to. He told me what realtor to contact and even told me which house I was going to get. He told me which agency to contact about employment. After I did everything he told me do. I put on my coat went on the internet one last time printed out the information

I needed to make my move. The answer was to move 1495 miles away from where I was. I got up I left my job didn't say bye to anyone. I walked out got in my van cried all the way back home to my mother's house. I cried so much I couldn't even see I had to pull over. I called my mother told her I had had enough and I just walked off my job and I was moving 1495 mile away. Now the move well my plan was to work at a temp agency and sell my house then move 1495 miles in a year or so. Well God plan was to not work in that city or live in that anymore and leave the next day. God had made his path for me he was just waiting for me to jump on and start traveling. I had no plan but the God that I serve and been praying to had finally gave me the solution I was waiting on. I tried to get a job at a temp agency for about 2 weeks before I left but I wasn't getting anywhere and I started getting frustrated. Even thou God had told me what to do I was scared. So I contacted a realtor to sell my house, map quested my directions to the new city. Took my van to the auto shop and made sure everything was working properly for the drive down there. We had just gotten a snow storm a few hours before I was to leave. I was so scared I was traveling alone in van with my oldest son to a place that I didn't know anything about didn't know what was ahead of me. I just knew I had to go there. I drove 24 hours straight I did not stop to sleep or rest only for gas. I drove through a snow storm, ice storm, hail, rain, and high winds until I got to my destination. So now God had stripped me of my man, house and my job. And he started restoring all that he had strip me of but made it better and greater than what I had before. I gotten a job with a company that people said I couldn't get into went from making $22,000 a year to making $52,000 a year. I brought me and my children a new house when people around me said I couldn't. 3600 square foot of house and I did it with God's help. My kids were blessed with a better school environment. Everybody's attitude changed for the better. I was only there 3 months and achieved all of that in 3 months. I can't tell you how many times I cried when I got here because I didn't know what in the hell I was going to do. I didn't know which directions I was going in I just knew that when I got to my destination that I would be okay. I don't think God would have let me come this far to fall down. He would not have wasted time talking to me if it was not to happen as he told me it would. I remember one day I was crying and we were staying at a hotel for a while until I had closed on my house. Things started off a little shaky. And I told my son I think it's better if we go back and his reply shocked the hell out of me he said "momma I don't know what the hell you are going to do but you will do something because we are not going back so stop crying". I couldn't even get mad at him for cussing at me. Because when I didn't have the strength left in me and no direction my child still had faith in me to make it happen for them like always.

But god isn't through stripping me just yet. I was mad at God for many years when I thought about all that I had gone through. Physically I was fine but emotionally and mentally I was screwed to the wall.

But no matter how dark the room is there is always some spick of light. I don't care if the room is 99.999999999% dark focus on the 0.0000000001% of light. I can't tell you how many times I been in that dark room locked up for seconds, minutes, hours and sometimes week at a time. I had so much pain inside that I couldn't see any light not even that 0.0000000001%. But I had to find that 0.0000000001% of light in order to survive. Sometimes I found it right away and sometimes it took a little longer to see. Even thou the situation look dark in your eyes it doesn't mean there isn't any light to be seen. But there are some people who never get out of the dark room and never learn to focus on that 0.000000001% of light to make it through. Even now when I find myself in the dark room I get in and get out quickly. I stay long enough to see what is in my life that is causing me darkness but I don't hang around long enough for it to consume me. Because God is my light in the dark room and my faith in him makes the light expand in my life. He is with me holding my hand and carrying me across the floor of darkness. So there is no reason for me to be afraid of the dark because the world doesn't stop cuz I am in pain.

If I had not endured all what had happened to me would I be this strong person that I am now? Would I know how to raise and provide for my children on my own like I've been doing? Would I even have faith in God in time of need or in time of happiness? He molded me to accept and deal with every pit fall and hole that was in my path of life. But a wound won't heal if you keep picking at it. He had to strip me of my mother. She didn't die but the relationship we had it had to end. I had to stop dealing with her at a close level because all she did was pick at my wounds and I would find myself hurting all over again with the same wounds I was begging God to heal. I begged God to get the visions and the negative feeling of my experience out of my mind and he did as I asked but every time I would start up a relationship with my mother and try to become close to her everything I prayed away came back. So I have to love her at a distance to heal myself. I had to cut down my own family tree and start my own with me being the roots. I know my relationship with her has walls and boundaries. Even now she can say her brother name in a conversation and I go into bi-polar mode on her. So I know I am not healed by what happened. And how she dealt with the situation definitely didn't help me any. It may not have helped her it just gave a way to not face it. Everything cannot always be swept under the rug.

I don't want anyone to hate my mother or have negative feelings towards her she is a good person in her own way. Her decisions that she made is something she has to deal with they will eat at her and not me. She made her choices that she felt would benefit her at the time. She is a great sister to her siblings. A great daughter to her mother. She is a wonderful grandmother to her grandchildren and a terrific mother to her adopted daughter. And a caring friend to some people. The best sister-n-law too many but to me she was just a person who help mold me into the person that I am today. I almost feel sorry for her my love she never wanted anymore. One day maybe she will want or need my love and affection will I be there? She always told me that everyone has to answer to God when they die. Everyone has to explain to him their actions they performed while living. I would just want to be a fly on the wall when she explains her actions towards me to God.

I didn't get a chance to become the veterinarian that I always wanted to become but that did not stop me from always trying to do something with my life regardless of the situation. I became a certified Dental Assistant, received my Personal Care Aide certificate, certified Nurse's Aide, a certificate for Teacher's Aide & Pharmacy Tech, and 2 associate degrees one in Micro-computers and one in Accounting and a 4 year degree in Business Management and Economics. I accomplished all of this on my own while being a single parent and dealing with my own emotional issues. The world doesn't stop because I am in pain the rotation doesn't stop so why should I. I still have to find a way to live my life regardless of how bad I am hurting the world isn't going to slow down for me or give me a chance to breathe. So I must find my own strength and fight for air. I am not saying don't deal with your issues because sooner or later they need to be dealt with either to heal you or for closure.

I don't know if I can ever find closure but sometimes healing is better than closure. I can't get closure because I will never fully understand why he did the things he did to me. He was given a road to travel one road was that he would have to ignore that evil desire in his heart that started this abuse. The other was to give in to the evil desire enjoy himself. Whenever you do wrong the outcome isn't always good. It may start out good because the devil has to blind you to make it seem like it is harmless and you can do whatever you want and never get caught and never pay for your sin. The devil is a liar!

Maybe if he would say sorry to me I could close the book on this and honestly forgive him from the bottom of heart and be able to get rid of all this hatred I have for him in my heart. But right now I just want to focus on the healing that I need. I had to find my own way to release and let go and heal. Like they say let go and let God. Because I couldn't let go of the pain and it was tearing me apart inside out. But God is stronger than me and he can do all things!

Part 6

My life is a testimony!

Wash me

Here I am standing here before you

With a tattered dirty white robe

And a dark but forgivable past

Here I am

Asking you to wash me

Here I am standing here before you

I have traveled my long dark journey

But I found you in the mist of my travels

Now I am asking you to wash me

Here I am

With the tears falling from my eyes

And my heart is crying out for mercy

Asking you to wash me

I had to let go and let God take it all. Sometimes we have to confront something head on. It's like slamming the door in Satan face. I had left the door open because I did not turn it over to God. Therefore the devil was free to come in and out as he pleased.

I had to accept the fact that my mother chose to protect a monster who in reality is her son. Maybe she felt I was strong enough to handle it and he wasn't man enough to face what he did. She lived in an era where it was common for women to give birth at home. No one could verify if you gave birth or not. It was mainly word of mouth. You reported it to the record keeping department or the mid-wife which during that era my great-grandmother was the towns midwife. She help to bring more than 75% of the town population into the world white and black. So yes my mother could have birth him into the world and yes another person could have taken him and claimed him as her own son. A black woman having a baby in a hospital was still on heard of in those days unless it was a black only hospital. And the closest hospital to that town is over an hour away. He may not even know who his real mother is. So part of this story can be a secret to him as well. Each person connected to the burying of the secret has been slowly dying little by little. Until they are either all dead or to old too tell the story. But all secrets get told. God has a way of exposing all things to the light.

I am thankful everyday that God gave me the strength to see the positive in my life regardless of how dark it began. I moved 1500 miles away and I began working my new job and then God placed some good people in my life as well. One of the ladies started a prayer circle at our job. We meeting up at noontime and we hold hands and pray. I had been baptized and I believed in God but I never opened up my mouth and prayed in front of other people. It was always alone when I prayed. Even at church I would hold hands with people but never got the urgue to open my mouth and verbally pray out loud what was in my heart. Everyone would hold hands and would say the names of the people in their household who they wanted covered in prayer. Then my co-worker would say a prayer for us all. Sometimes I would cry and sometimes I wouldn't. Then one day my co-worker wasn't feeling good and she didn't feel like praying over us and she asked me to do the prayer. I was scared to death. Pray how in God's name do I pray over people? That day I opened my mouth and I prayed from my soul for the first time in my life. I did like she told me "speak from your heart". That is the day I got saved. You don't have to be in church to get saved. There are seven days in a week and God can save you any day at any moment anywhere. That day I felt God work all through me that day. My body felt like it was on fire but I wasn't burning. God's touch brought me to my knees and I remember my co-workers holding me up and I kept praying and the tearing just flowed from my eyes and some snot to. I let go and let God and I let him into my soul to heal me and save me. That day everyone cried we had all been touched by God. When two or more gather he said he will be in the midst. And he was.

That day I learned to use my dark past as a testimony. The situation was dark but it didn't keep me down. I still overcame everything the devil threw at me. I am a woman a great woman! I began sending out testimonies everyday to the group using my own life challenges to support the Word.

Proverbs 31 10:11
10 A wife of noble character who can find? She is worth far more than rubies.
11 Her husband has full confidence in her and lacks nothing of value.

"Us as women we sometimes seem to doubt our worth or value if we don't stand up to a certain standard or WIFE code. I felt that since I was abused I would never be good enough to be a wife to some. Before I got good with God it didn't matter what type of women I was. I was a woman a pretty woman and that was all that mattered to me. I knew my looks could get me far in life but I learn quickly that looks aren't everything. Throughout my life from the beginning my father was trying to mold me into the woman in Proverbs 31. He knew what she was and I think about our time together and how he was slowly teaching me how to be her even thou I had faults.

Here are some of the characteristics of the Proverbs 31 Woman

1. ***Virtue. Proverbs 31:10***
2. ***Faithfulness. Proverbs 31:11***
3. ***Reverence. Proverbs 31:12***
4. ***Goodness. Proverbs 31:12***
5. ***Willing Worker. Proverbs 31:13***
6. ***Good Manager. Proverbs 31:14,15***
7. ***Industrious. Proverbs 31:16***
8. ***Strength. Proverbs 31:17***
9. ***Endurance. Proverbs 31:18***
10. ***Well Rounded. Proverbs 31:19***
11. ***Charitable. Proverbs 31:20***
12. ***Provider. Proverbs 31:21***
13. ***Well Dressed. Proverbs 31:22***
14. ***Wife of a Good Husband. Proverbs 31:23***
15. ***Good Business Woman. Proverbs 31:24***
16. ***Honorable. Proverbs 31:25***
17. ***Wise. Proverbs 31:26a***
18. ***Kind. Proverbs 31:26b***
19. ***Good Mother. Proverbs 31:27a***

20. ***Busy. Proverbs 31:27b***
21. ***Praiseworthy. Proverbs 31:28***
22. ***Attains or Excels. Proverbs 31:29***
23. ***Fear of the Lord. Proverbs 31:30***
24. ***Fruit bearing. Proverbs 31:31***

I am not perfect. Early in my life I experience abuse from my uncle. But my father not for one moment felt that I was not a good woman. He taught me the importance of being a good woman of being a good wife to someone one day. He talked to me about money how to make sure you have enough to cover your bills take what you have a make work. He reminded me to stop and think about every situation. How your actions affect the household. He told me to be kind to people and help others would I could. I learned how to be a good mother by taking care of the foster kids my parents had. I learned how to fear the Lord early in life and even thou my father was a womanizer he always got on me whenever I came over wearing something to revealing "Go upstairs and get one of my old t-shirts" he would tell me. I was not allowed to wear no booty shirts, no mini- skirts, no shirts revealing cleavage it didn't matter about me being grown up until the day he died I always had to dress a certain way around my father. All these things that make a perfect wife he put into me from the day I born until the day he died. I have a touch of every characteristic that makes up a perfect wife some touches are more abundant than others but they are still there. Look at yourself women I am sure you have a touch of every characteristic. And if you have a touch of something that is not on the list then you need to x it out your life! **A wife of noble character who can find? She is worth far more than rubies** I thank God for taking me little old me. He took my dark past and still took time to shape me into the perfect woman in Proverbs 31. The devil had me fooled for a long time had me thinking I was nothing but the dirt on the bottom of your shoe. He had me thinking I was nothing he had me wanting to kill myself he even has my Christian family members talking bad about me but today I realized that through it all GOD has formed me into the woman of Proverbs 31!! I was molested but yet my God still continued to work with me and form me into the woman of Proverbs 31! I was raped but yet my God thought I was still good enough to become the woman of Proverbs 31! I tried to kill myself but yet my God let me live to become the woman of Proverbs 31! I wanted to give up but yet my God gave me strength to become the woman of Proverbs 31! Many have turned their backs on me and talked about me but my God still molded me into the woman of Proverbs 31! I had children out of wedlock they each have a different father but my God still felt I was good enough to be molded into the woman of Proverbs 31! See it don't matter what others say or think about you or even do to you. If GOD think that you fit the puzzle then no matter what is against you YOU will fit in that puzzle!! We cannot let the outside world influence us to think otherwise BEAUTY is in the EYES of the BEHOLDER and the BEHOLDER is GOD!! My own mother calls me tramps, whores and every other name you can think of yet she is a Christian woman and growing up hearing that cut me deeply but in the EYES of my FATHER my GOD he saw I was the woman for Proverbs 31! I am not perfect I still have issues I now know that I carry each of these characteristics inside of me and I know that the ones that I carry that are not on this list has got to go!! We are all women of Proverbs 31 just look at yourself look at the things that you have gone through. I am sure that you earned one or more of these characteristics after you won the battle with the devil! The closer I get to God the more these characteristics shine in my soul the more they come out in my life and through the things I do. And before you know that dark part you had will be gone. You will even forget it is there. We didn't start off perfect but during our ordeals in life God made us into the woman of Proverbs 31! And we have to teach our daughters and granddaughters and any other young woman that is influenced by us that through the storm and the battles God will still turn you into the perfect woman if you let him come into your life and guide you! **A wife of noble character who can find? She is worth far more than rubies**. Her husband has full confidence in her and lacks nothing of value. Look deep inside yourself and find the Proverbs 31 woman inside of you I did!

My life is a testimony. God has given me the strength to use and talk about my past to give people hope and to help them keep their faith in him. I was no longer ashamed of my past because there is nothing to be ashamed of once I let go and let God. I had to use that darkness and turn it into light and salvation. I could not let this situation in my life destroy me. It had almost killed that little girl inside of me there are only remnants of her in my memory that are untouched by him that dwell in my heart. And that is where I keep her safe.

It is not easy. There are days were I want to be touched, hugged and kissed on. And there are days that I don't want anything to touch me at all. Not even the kisses from my own children.

1 Peter 2:3

2 Like newborn babies, crave pure spiritual milk, so that by it you may grow up in your salvation, 3 now that you have tasted that the Lord is good.

"Have you ever gotten a taste of something good? Like a good piece of chocolate cake or some good tender ribs? And even thou it may not have been good for your health you ate it anyway because it tasted so good. The Lord was feeding me all along. I was drinking his milk through the blessing he was giving me in my life. And I didn't know at the time what it was that I was drinking. I was just in taking the blessing at hand but not understanding them fully. **1 Peter 2 Like newborn babies, crave pure spiritual milk, so that by it you may grow up in your salvation, 3 now that you have tasted that the Lord is good**. I did not know what it was I was drinking until I realized that I was saved. When I broke down and cried out to the Lord and began to thank him over and over again for what he has done for me. I then realized the MILK I had been drinking all these years was good. And I didn't run I didn't walk away. I had to start reading the word and talking about the word with you because I got a good taste of that milk and I cannot go another step *without it! **1 Peter*** **2 Like newborn babies, crave pure spiritual milk, so that by it you may grow up in your salvation, 3 now that you have tasted that the Lord is good**. I was sipping on the milk. OH my bills are paid. Oh I have food to eat. Oh I have clothes to wear! Oh this and Oh that but I had to be put in a situation where I was naked. I had to be stripped naked. It was a lot harder to get the Oh that and oh this done! It took a lot longer for the Oh that and oh this to happen. My milk supply was running out. I had to cry out to HIM that was my only choice. And I had to think about my blessing and that milk that I received was just a small taste of the Lord. And my soul knew I love it. I shed a few tears I guess the Lord knew I was holding out so some more things had to happen to me. So then I started to cry but only a little bit the Lord knew I was holding out. So some more things had to happen. Then I started to weep a little bit the Lord knew I was holding out so He held on to His milk. Then I cried a little bit then a little snot came with the tears and God knew I was still holding back so some more things had to happen to me. Then finally I broke down completely cried, screamed, weeped, snot everywhere and tears falling like a waterfall. I was on my knees I let it all go because I wanted that milk I had tasted the Lord. I knew what it was like to have HIM in my life I had to get HIM back! **1 Peter 2 Like newborn babies, crave pure spiritual milk, so that by it you may grow up in your salvation, 3 now that you have tasted that the Lord is good**. If you feel like God is just giving you a taste of the milk like you are drinking out of a baby bottle change something in your life. The baby bottle is good but once you realize that you can get more than sipping that God can give you a big jug of milk and you can just toss it back like shot glass change your life to get it. You may have to lose some people that are close to you in order to get it. It is up to you to choose what it is you want. I was glad that God decided to save me and cover me with his spiritual milk and cover my body, guide my steps, calm my heart and clear my mind. Every day I try to think up ways to keep my supply up. I don't want to be on my knees again begging the Lord to have mercy on me. Jesus has already died for me so I don't have to beg. God said all I have to do is ask and it shall be given because. My supply of milk is on full I have tasted the Lord and the Lord was good I will never let my supply of milk get on empty again. I know how it is to walk around with no milk that is just like eating cereal with water."

I had to realize that I was still worthy of God's love. I was mad at God for a moment in life. I couldn't understand why he would let something like that happen to me. But God's will is not for me to understand. I had to stop wondering on the why it happened but concentrating on how I made it through the ordeal. Maybe I had to suffer so that my children wouldn't have to. I don't know the reason I am just glad I can use my life as a testimony. I am glad that I am able to testify and use my life as a testimony to others. When God saved me I knew at that moment that I had been dressed in my white robe. It didn't matter about the past 36 years of my life. God had wiped the slate clean and healed me on the spot!

Revelation 7 13:17

13 Then one of the elders asked me, "These in white robes—who are they, and where did they come from?"

14 I answered, "Sir, you know."

And he said, "These are they who have come out of the great tribulation; they have washed their robes and made them white in the blood of the Lamb. 15 Therefore,

"They are before the throne of God and serve him day and night in his temple; and he who sits on the throne will shelter them with his presence. 16 'Never again will they hunger; never again will they thirst. The sun will not beat down on them,' nor any scorching heat. 17 For the Lamb at the center of the throne will be their shepherd; 'he will lead them to springs of living water.' 'And God will wipe away every tear from their eyes.'

"I use to wear dirty clothes! They were brand new from the store may have even went to the cleaners and got them pressed and starch but they were dirty! Because the person wearing them had not been washed in the blood of the Lamb! I am happy that God decided to have mercy on me and save me that day across the street at the park July 2011 my dirty clothes were washed with the blood of the Lamb I felt in my soul that I was truly SAVED and forgiven. 13 **Then one of the elders asked me, "These in white robes—who are they, and where did they come from?"14 I answered, "Sir, you know."And he said, "These are they who have come out of the great tribulation; they have washed their robes and made them white in the blood of the Lamb.** Yes you are going through some things right now but the after the storm you will be sitting in heaven with Jesus wearing all white! Dirt can't touch you no more!! Yes it is hard but it won't always be that way and the reward is great! No matter what it is that you are going through you have to have faith in God that you will make it you have to make it so you can be washed in the blood! **"These are they who have come out of the great tribulation; they have washed their robes and made them white in the blood of the Lamb.** I remember when God touched me hottest thing I ever felt it was menopause times 1 million! God was putting that white robe on me! I have to keep that in mind that regardless of what you see me wearing I have to represent this white robe I have on underneath! He touched me to let me know I was saved I was forgiven your slate is washed clean it is up to me to keep it clean and keep making choices that represent him and honor him and give him glory! I am not perfect that is why God give us strength and faith and the Holy Spirit to work with us if we let it!! Satan wants you to think you're not wearing white you are if you have been saved by God and washed in the blood then you have on a white robe and don't let Satan trick you into dirting up your robe! **"These are they who have come out of the great tribulation; they have washed their**

robes and made them white in the blood of the Lamb. I am not perfect I have to wash my robe through asking God for forgiveness! I have to sew up a few holes by depending on my faith! I have to put some starch guard on it by covering myself with the Holy Spirit! And God makes my robe shine by pour down blessing on me! **"These are they who have come out of the great tribulation; they have washed their robes and made them white in the blood of the Lamb**. When you got saved! When you got Baptised! When you decided to turn your life over to God! When you started activating your faith your temple inside your chest! When you cried out and asked God for forgiveness! When you claimed Jesus as your Shepard you were putting on your white robe!"

I couldn't move on in my life because I had too many open wounds that needed to be healed. Writing my life experience down has helped me to heal a lot. Maybe one day while I am going down this road of healing I can get my mother back. We can be close again maybe she will say she loves me or even hug or allow me to kiss her on the cheek again.

We are not able to choose who our parents will be. Life is like a deck of cards and you have to be able to work with the cards you are dealt and make the best of it. Every now and then you have to be able to put a card down and pick up a new one. But when you put that card down make sure you don't need it anymore. Because in a card game you can't go back and pick it back up again once you have thrown it down. My mother is still in my hand while I try to build me a full house. Even thou there is animosity and anger present between us I have to be the bigger person and find that 0.000000001% of light in the relationship to make it better between us. If not for us then for own myself. This is something we both have to overcome so we both can heal. She is also a victim of this situation in her own way whether she wants to admit it or not.

> **Isaiah 26 1:4**
> **We have a strong city; God makes salvation its walls and ramparts. 2 Open the gates that the righteous nation may enter, the nation that keeps faith. 3 You will keep in perfect peace those whose minds are steadfast, because they trust in you. 4 Trust in the Lord forever, for the Lord, the Lord himself, is the Rock eternal.**

4 **Trust in the Lord forever, for the Lord, the Lord himself, is the Rock eternal**. When you see a rock on the ground do you ever think of the life of the rock? How long as that rock been on the earth? Was that rock here when the earth was formed? Scientist can dig deep into the earth and pull up a rock that is dated back billions of years back to when God first formed the earth!**4 Trust in the Lord forever, for the Lord, the Lord himself, is the Rock eternal.** You know that over time a small pebble can accumulate layers that make it bigger and the pebble somehow become a large boulder and then that boulder form mountains that never seem to crumble! Now I look at my faith. I think when I started out it was smaller than a mustard seed maybe even microscopic! And over time those battles that I won because I had God fighting for me

and it is impossible for God to lose a battle so seeing that I never lost a battle those winnings that I had accumulated over time caused my microscopic seed to get some layers!! But those layers only formed when I recognized what it was that God was doing in my life! **4 Trust in the Lord forever, for the Lord, the Lord himself, is the Rock eternal.** Are you with me? Okay let's roll on! Now that my seed is about the size of a kidney bean and seeing that from time to time it varies in size! Today it could be a kidney bean tomorrow it could be a mustard seed and next week it could be an avocado seed! I had to take my seed and from a rock around it!**4 Trust in the Lord forever, for the Lord, the Lord himself, is the Rock eternal.** The word helped me form that rock around my seed! A rock of strength from the Lord that will never crumble! A rock that will continue to get bigger and bigger in size over time with the word! God gave us the word to help form that rock around your seed!!**4 Trust in the Lord forever, for the Lord, the Lord himself, is the Rock eternal. I had to get that word!** God gave us the word for a reason to help you build your rock! You can break a rock down to a sand pebble and over time layer upon layer builds up around that sand pebble until it becomes so big that you can't even drill to the small sand pebble on the bottom! The word is helping us build our Godly rock the rock eternal! No matter what the devil does he will never be able to crush your rock out of existence! He may break it into pieces but the word will help you build it up again! He may chip away at it but the word will help you build up another layer! He may try to crumble it but the word will build you up again! **4 Trust in the Lord forever, for the Lord,**

the Lord himself, is the Rock eternal. Look at the dinosaurs they long gone but the rocks from that time period are still here! All those ancient civilizations are gone but the rocks they left behind are still here! Stonehenge still here! Gaza pyramids in Egypt still here! They even found meteorite fragments from millions of years ago still here! Fossil from the first living organism from billions of years ago still here! The Ten Commandments written in stone still here we are still following them! So what makes you think that the Rock eternal won't be here for you? I hope that the rock I am building is strong enough for my children so when I am dead and gone that my children can take my rock and build upon it! **4 Trust in the Lord forever, for the Lord, the Lord himself, is the Rock eternal.**

I can't tell you how to heal because every situation is different and everyone deals with pain differently. But I can tell you in order to feel good about yourself you have to take something positive out of every negative situation you incur in your life. And if their isn't something positive in the situation then you make some positive happen. I had to deal with molestation, rape, suicide, hate, and neglect, lies, depression, loneliness , betrayal, insecurities and probably a few more things that I over looked or just don't have a name for. But I always had to focus on the positive. You can never let the negative outweigh the positive. If you get overtaken by the negative it will eat you up and spit you out and then run you over. Negative energy can make you do negative things to yourself and sometimes to people close to you. I am still dealing with a lot inside that I don't show or tell. I know that my mind is not completely anger free and speaking to a counselor again is not in my immediate future. They say just find a quiet place and pray. I pray every day sometimes at work across the street in the little park. I sit on the bench and just talk to God and beg him to keep my mind focused and heal me where I need to be healed. So far I am healing slowly but surely. Prayer is more promising and safer for me.

God has already taken everything away from me in order to heal me like I asked the only thing left is the void in my heart that I feel.

Like I said before I don't want anyone to hate my mother. She was a good wife to my father. She is a terrific grandmother to my children. She is a good daughter to her mother. And she is a great sister to her siblings. She is a nice aunt to her nieces and nephews and their children. And she was the best mother ever to me for the first 14 years of my life. Now that I am almost a senior citizen I am still trying to rebuild that close relationship we once had when I was a child. I want to feel love from her not tolerated. I have felt that way for too long.

No matter what I went through what I am going through right now and what I have to face in my future I still believe that God protected me and covered me through it all even when I was in the dark room. My life didn't start off so great but that doesn't mean it has to remain that way. I have to find a way to take this negative beginning of my life and turn it into a positive ending.

The little girl in me died in 1977. Her long pony tails and wide smile was buried under the covers of a monster. I don't know how she really was or what she would have become if she would have had her mother's love in her life. If she would have kept her innocence and not have it stolen away. Would I be where I am today had that little girl lived her life or would I be somewhere else more happy less depressed maybe even hear "I love you" on a regular basis from my mother. Whoever that little girl was she vanished and her memory is something I have to learn to let go and let the person I have become try and live and try to survive.

Acts 7 51:60

51 "You stiff-necked people! Your hearts and ears are still uncircumcised. You are just like your ancestors: You always resist the Holy Spirit! 52 Was there ever a prophet your ancestors did not persecute? They even killed those who predicted the coming of the Righteous One. And now you have betrayed and murdered him— 53 you who have received the law that was given through angels but have not obeyed it."

54 When the members of the Sanhedrin heard this, they were furious and gnashed their teeth at him.55 But Stephen, full of the Holy Spirit, looked up to heaven and saw the glory of God, and Jesus standing at the right hand of God. 56 "Look," he said, "I see heaven open and the Son of Man standing at the right hand of God."

57 At this they covered their ears and, yelling at the top of their voices, they all rushed at him, 58 dragged him out of the city and began to stone him. Meanwhile, the witnesses laid their coats at the feet of a young man named Saul.

59 While they were stoning him, Stephen prayed, "Lord Jesus, receive my spirit." 60 Then he fell on his knees and cried out, "Lord, do not hold this sin against them." When he had said this, he fell asleep.

Act 8:1

And Saul approved of their killing him.

" Sometimes you have to let Jesus put you to sleep in order for HIM to work it out for you! You know the saying let go and let God! When you are praying to God you don't know how he is going to answer you but you know that you will get answered by HIM! Sometimes God has to put your conscious mind to sleep in order for the subconscious mind to take over which is the HOLY SPIRIT inside of you! Have you ever looked back at some of the things you have done and couldn't believe that you did it? God put you to sleep! He heard you but he had to put you to sleep in order to answer your pray! Yes it was you walking! Yes it was you talking! Yes it was you doing all of those marvelous things but God had to put you to sleep in order to get it done**! 59 While they were stoning him, Stephen prayed, "Lord Jesus, receive my spirit." 60 Then he fell on his knees and cried out, "Lord, do not hold this sin**

against them." When he had said this, he fell asleep. Stephen was being stoned to death and he did not want them to have his spirit so he prayed and Jesus answered him! Jesus took his spirit and put Stephen to sleep! Even thou Stephen body was going to die Jesus had already taken his spirit so Stephen body was lifeless whatever torture they did to it Jesus had saved Stephen from it because he PRAYED!! **59 While they were stoning him, Stephen prayed, "Lord Jesus, receive my spirit." 60 Then he fell on his knees and cried out, "Lord, do not hold this sin against them." When he had said this, he fell asleep**. When you have the spirit working on your behalf you can do all things through Christ that strengthen you! **55 But Stephen, full of the Holy Spirit, looked up to heaven and saw the glory of God, and Jesus standing at the right hand of God. 56 "Look," he said, "I see heaven open and the Son of Man standing at the right hand of God**." They were stoning him and dragging him through the streets and hitting him and calling him terrible names but through it all he KEPT his eye on Jesus! You have to go through some rough times but you have to remember to keep your eye on Jesus! Stephan was so full of the spirit that he probably didn't even know they were dragging him through the streets he was focused on Jesus! **56 "Look," he said, "I see heaven open and the Son of Man standing at the right hand of God."57 At this they covered their ears and, yelling at the top of their voices, they all rushed**

at him, 58 dragged him out of the city and began to stone him.

Not only do you have to pray but you have to stay focused on Jesus! Sometimes you cannot worry about the people dragging you through the streets all you have to do is stay focused on Jesus and he will work it out in your favor! Your body can be ran over, torn to pieces, set on fire, mutilated but as long as you don't get my spirit the things you do to my body means nothing!! My spirit is for the LORD and the LORD only! I think about the times I was molested and raped they took my body but they never TOOK my spirit and that is how I made it through! Jesus had to put me to sleep to make sure I made it through! He woke me up when all the destruction was over! He woke me up when I was able to handle it! He woke me up when all the enemies were gone! He woke me up after the devil had left me for dead! The devil tortured my body but he never got my soul! It don't matter what they do to the body as long as the devil don't get your soul! Your soul can never die and that is why the devil wants it! Sometimes you have to let Jesus put you to sleep to work it out so the Devil don't get it**! 59 While they were stoning him, Stephen prayed, "Lord Jesus, receive my spirit." 60 Then he fell on his knees and cried out, "Lord, do not hold this sin against them." When he had said this, he fell asleep.** Stephen took time out before Jesus put him to sleep to pray for his enemies! Love thy enemies like you love yourself! Stephen is a great example of that! They were about to stone him to death but he still prayed for them! He still asked Jesus to forgive them! How many enemies have you prayed for?

It has been 3 years since I have spoken to my mother and 42 months since I have been saved. Over 2 years ago I finally changed her contact information in my phone for her. It went from mommy to her name.

A little over 3 years has passed and her name shows up in my phone one day. Right away I knew it was an emergency. My first mind said hit the ignore button. But that decision was out of anger. I had been trying to call her throughout the years not once did she accept my phone calls. Not once did she respond to my text messages. And sending message to me through my children was childish but that was her way of not accepting reality. My heart decided to answer the phone to see if she has broken down and called me then it must be a life and death situation. I answered and she proceeded to tell me that my big momma the only person other than my children who I knew in my heart had unconditional love for me, had been in the hospital for the past 6 weeks with an undiagnosed aliment. And that she and her sister were leaving the next day to go see her because it was not looking so good. She said she would call me to give me updates on her condition. And she kept her word. She called me every other day to give me updates but once she had made a recovery the phone calls stopped as quickly as they began. But this time I didn't get upset I didn't get depressed. I didn't go chasing after her. Instead I was happy that I could be there for her and give her comfort during her upsetting time. Even though I had never received that comfort from her during my life time.

One day I was going through something in my life. God never said the road would be easy,but that he would give you relief along the way. I needed to pray to God and I decided to go to the park on my lunch break. The place where I had been saved at 42 months ago. I was dressed in a beige business suit, black heels and my hair was looking flawless. I threw my hands up to the blue skies and went into prayer while standing in the park. And I saw a young woman approaching me. I could tell by her clothing she was homeless. She walked towards me and the first thing that came to my mind was that she is about to ask me for money. And I didn't even have my purse on me today. But she approached me and said "excuse me but can you pray for me like you just did? I don't know how to pray but I need someone to pray for me. And I was watching you as you prayed." I told her of course I could. It wasn't a problem.

I didn't know how old she was but I could tell by her voice that she was of Spanish decent. I asked her what her name was. And she told me "Ruby". I held her hands and began praying for her. I said a few words it only lasted about a minute. When I was finished she said "can you pray for me again? I have done so much bad in my life that God won't listen to me." I asked her if she had been baptized or christened. And she said “yes”. I asked her if she had accepted Jesus Christ as her Lord and savior. And she said “yes”. I said do you believe he died for you and rose from the dead? And she said “yes”. I gave her a confused look and started praying for her again this time it was a little longer than the first prayer. When I was finished she said “I want to pray like you. Teach me to pray like you.”Now I have even a more confused look on my face. I told her okay and told her the first thing you have to do is repent. She asked “well what is that?”. I said you must confess to God of all the bad things that you have done during your lifetime so far. She took a deep breath and started crying. I held her hands as she began. She started asking for forgiveness for her drug use for the past 9 years. She stated every drug that she had used. Some I had never even heard of before. She asked God to forgive her for selling herself for money to buy drugs. She began asking God to forgive her for robbing people and assaulting people for drug money. She asked God to forgive her for the way she been treating her parents,and for all the pain she had caused them. She asked to be forgiven for not being a good mom to her little girl. I finally asked her how old she was and she said 21. I was shocked because she had been doing drugs since she was 12 and she looked so much older. I was assuming that was around 30 years of age. I told her that since she had repented of her sins that God was ready to help her. I also told her that whenever you do something wrong confess it to Him like you just did and ask for forgiveness and ask Him to give you strength so that you never repeat it. I held her hands tight and I told her the first thing you do is thank God for waking you up. Regardless of where you woke up at and the condition you are in thank Him for waking you up. And tell Him what you need or want and He will honor you prayer. Make sure your words are sincere and your heart is sincere as well. And keep yourself humble to Him.

She began to pray some of it was in Spanish. I do not know Spanish but I said "amen" and "please bless her Father". She wept and continued praying and I kept holding her hands until she was done.

By now it was way over my lunch break and I didn't care. All I cared about at that particular moment was her. I got some tissue out of my pocket and wiped her face off. And she looked at me and said "why are you giving up your time to help?" I looked at her and said "what do you see?" and she said "I can tell by your clothes that you must have a nice job and it must be important." I started laughing and said "honey this outfit is from a garage sale. The whole outfit including the shoes cost me about $3.00. Now I am about to tell you what you don't see".

We walked over to a nearby bench and sat down. I told her the story of my life the story that you just read. Her reply to me after I was finished was "how is it that you can smile"? I told her once God healed me all the pain went away. Now I have no choice but to smile. I still go through difficult times in my life but I keep on smiling. And after that I gave her a big hug. I told her my address and "said if you need me come find me". I pointed to the building across the street and told her that is where I work. And you can go to the front desk and ask me.

A few weeks went by and I felt that I would never hear from her. I keep lifting her name up in prayer. And one day I received a letter in the mail from her. She had been incarnated but because of our encounter in the park she was doing great mentally and emotionally. She told me that ever since we meant that she has been praying to God on a regular and felt really good about herself. She asked me to continue praying for her and to write her back as soon as I could. I hurried up and compiled some prayers and scriptures together the ones that I had been sending out to the prayer group. I packed them in an envelope. I placed two stamps on the envelope. Because it was 10 pages and was a little heavy. I mailed it off and two weeks later I get a reply from her again. She said she loved my prayers and so did everyone else in the P.O.D she was in. And if it wasn't too much could I please send them some more. She was part of a prayer circle there and they were using my prayers in their group study. So I ran over to the computer compiled the ones together that I had sent out over the past two weeks and mailed them off to her.

Receiving her letters gave me so much joy. Knowing that God took my negative situation, and turned it around and allowed me to use it as a positive felt great because I had made it through.

Just knowing that my story help to save one person gives me joy. I would not rewrite my life for nothing in the world. It made me and I love being me.

If you cannot let go of the pain from the past it will forever hold you in bondage. It is so important to forgive yourself. Also forgive the person who caused it. I never forgave my family personally for their actions, but I threw my hands up to the sky and confessed forgiveness for them with my mouth and my heart to God. In an instant all the pain went away and I was free.

I don't let my past bother me. I just let it bother the people who can't let it go.

Thank you Dwight it takes a strong man to love a broken woman.

www.ingramcontent.com/pod-product-compliance
Lightning Source LLC
Chambersburg PA
CBHW051821040426
42447CB00006B/314